THINK ON THESE

PHILIPPIANS 4:8

think on
† these

A Study of Philippians 4:8

HEIDI GOEHMANN

I Love My Shepherd

Sources used:
Biblegateway.com, multiple translations
Biblehub.com interlinear Greek/Hebrew
Matthew Henry Commentary
The Lutheran Study Bible from Concordia Publishing House

ISBN:1536928631
ISBN-13:978-1536928631

I'm so glad you've decided to join me on a journey of study surrounding **Philippians 4:8**. This passage has lots of great insight, both theologically and practically- that is, for study to simply know and understand God more, as well as to use in our everyday life.

This is an eight week devotional study with five days of study per week. Each day has readings and some of the days have questions for personal exploration. These exploration questions will not appear everyday, in order to give you some time to simply rest in the Word. The study can be used as a personal study or devotional, or it is appropriate for group study also. For a group setting, I suggest you discuss a few of the study readings that stuck with you, and share your thoughts from some of the exploration questions for the week. Groups might alternatively do one or two days of the devotions together in community, and then complete the other three or four days on their own.

The study is meant to be hands-on. Get your Bible, your colored pens, and highlighters out. Mark up your Bible, write in the margins of this study, and answer the questions as you go along. There is a lot of white space in the pages intentionally - write or doodle wherever you see fit to engage in the Scriptures. Be sure to check out the Scripture Engagement tools related to the study at ilovemyshepherd.com. Simply go to the site, click on Studies Available and look for the Think on These tab.

Each week there is also a ***heart verse*** at the beginning of the study. This verse is meant to be studied, jotted down, post-it noted, slapped somewhere prominent in your home, memorized or anything that will help the verse settle deep in your heart.

I am blessed that you have picked up this study. Dear Lord, guide this precious reader, speak to them through Your Word, fill their heart with joy. Fill their minds with new insights and understanding of Your great love for Your children. In Jesus Name I pray, Amen.

Remember, sister, He is true. He is honorable. He is just. He is pure. He is lovely. He is commendable. He is excellent. He is most worthy of praise.

Blessings to you as you study!

Heidi ♡

week one

Truth

God speaks Truth
Jesus is Truth
The Spirit is Truth
The world really does care about Truth
We can speak Truth to a hurting world

heart verse

a verse to meditate on for the week, to post somewhere, or to memorize:

"...and you will know the truth, and the truth will set you free."

John 8:32

Day 1
God speaks Truth

Truth in our culture is a difficult thing. Moral relativism and postmodern, or post Christian, culture tell us constantly that one person's truth may be different from another's. These kinds of thoughts pervade our media, the Internet, and our Facebook feeds. They proclaim that a loving God blesses all unions formed from love, abortion is an option, and hurtful words spoken with good intentions are good words. How do we as Christians respond to this in our own little spot on this planet? How do we know what to focus on, what ideas to share, and how to engage in the discussion without losing Love on one hand or Truth on the other?

We can begin with a firm foundation of what Truth really is and where we can turn to find it. So, let's do just that! Let's dig in.

The Greek word for truth in this passage is *alethe* which can mean unconcealed, true in fact, truthful, or literally what can't be hidden. *It is undeniable reality when something can not be hidden or concealed.*

First, consider, off the top of your head…what about God do you consider in your heart to be undeniable reality? Jot some notes in the margin or in a journal. Let that sit a moment.

Let's look at Isaiah 45:18-19 (emphasis added by the author).

> *For thus says the LORD,*
> *who created the heavens*
> * (he is God!),*
> *who formed the earth and made it*
> * (he established it;*
> *he did not create it empty,*
> * he formed it to be inhabited!):*
> *"I am the LORD, and there is no other.*
> ***I did not speak in secret,***
> * in a land of darkness;*
> *I did not say to the offspring of Jacob,*
> * 'Seek me in vain.'*
> *I the LORD **speak the truth;***
> * I declare what is right.*

God begins v. 19 by proclaiming, *"I did not speak in secret"* comparing secret to darkness. And finishes the verse with a firm *"I the Lord speak truth."*

God is trustworthy! All that He says is plain, not ambiguous or through priests and oracles, like the pagans did in Isaiah's time. On Mt. Sinai God spoke clearly to His people and to us. He appeared to Abraham, Isaac, Jacob, and more.

Ephesians 1:13-14 continues to ensure us that the entire Word is God's spoken Truth. We can fully trust it as the Gospel of our salvation.

> *In him you also, when you heard the word of truth, the gospel of your salvation, and believed in him, were sealed with the promised Holy Spirit, who is the guarantee of our inheritance until we acquire possession of it, to the praise of his glory.*

We have His Word, laid out for us, to search and discern any question. God does not conceal anything from us. We can search His Word to find Truth, whenever we are questioning. We can check what we hear, read, and see with His Word. His Word is a Gift and an active part of salvation working in our lives daily.

Exploration
What about the Word being "not hidden" or "spoken plainly", by God Himself, makes it more trustworthy?

See John 8:32. What does this verse tell us of truth?

Has anyone ever hidden anything from you and left you uncomfortable or distrusting? (This can be deep and profound or something like finding out that Santa is not real.)

Day 2
Jesus is Truth

We know it in our hearts. Jesus is Truth. But when the voices of the world press in, what passages can we stand on to remind us-He IS Truth itself? He and no other! No thing, no height nor depth of thinking is truth, outside of Him.

We can find ourselves with questions flitting through our mind, ranging from "What if some other religion is the one that is right? What if we're all right and it doesn't really matter what name we use for God?" to "Is Jesus enough? Do I need something else? What if I missed something somewhere?"

Perhaps you have never particularly struggled with these kinds of questions in your soul, but there are those around you who do, and being aware of the difficult questions prepares us when difficult times come that shake the ground we stand on. So let's stand in Truth together!

John 1:14-17
>   *And the Word became flesh and dwelt among us, and we have seen his glory, glory as of the only Son from the Father, full of grace and truth. (John bore witness about him, and cried out, "This was he of whom I said, 'He who comes after me ranks before me, because he was before me.'") For from his fullness we have all received, grace*

upon grace. For the law was given through Moses; grace and truth came through Jesus Christ.

"Jesus full of grace and truth…"
"grace and truth came through Jesus…"

Do you see the sandwich ends of this passage with all the nutrients of grace served up in the middle? This passage couples beautifully the natures of Jesus. He is fully Truth and fully Grace all wrapped into the perfect Son of God, laid in a manger, wrapped in burial clothes, robed in radiance, on the right hand of God. When we worry and wonder about Truth, this passage reminds us that not only Truth, but Grace upon Grace flows out of Jesus to us. Even when we fail to see truth, to live truth, to speak truth. Grace wraps us up, to die and rise with Him.

Now let's look at John 14:6.
> *Jesus said to him, "I am the way, and the truth, and the life. No one comes to the Father except through me."*

These verses again cement for us that Jesus is Truth and Truth comes through Him. We are often wondering and looking all around us for answers to questions, for directions in life. What we really are searching for is truth - the truth of what matters, what our purpose is, how we can make a difference. We need look no further, sisters. Turn to Him; He fills in all the blanks. He is always, always the answer.

<u>Exploration</u>
How do you begin to discern something when you need to make a decision?

What Bible passages have you found in moments of looking for truth?

Day 3
The Spirit is Truth

Last year my husband and I read the book "Forgotten God" by Francis Chan on audiobook for our nightly devotion together. This isn't a plug for that book, but the premise is that within the church, we hardly ever talk about the third person of the Trinity- the Holy Spirit. This really resonated with my husband and me. I think this largely has to do with the mystery of the work of the Spirit. We know what the Spirit does- gives saving Faith, a gift in our baptisms, working through the Word as the Sword of the Spirit, but I'm speaking of the mystery of *how* the Spirit works. Even while stating firmly "In baptism!", there is still a mystery to the work of the Spirit in our hearts and lives.

We love and hate a good mystery. We want to KNOW.
The good news – Scripture does not leave out the Spirit when talking about truth!

The Gospel of John brings up the matter of truth over and over again. Let's take another look.

John 14:16-18
> *And I will ask the Father, and he will give you*
> *another Helper, to be with you forever, even the Spirit of*
> *truth, whom the world cannot receive, because it neither*
> *sees him nor knows him. You know him, for he dwells with*

you and will be in you. I will not leave you as orphans; I will come to you.

This passage tells us

→ The Spirit is truth. Just like the Father. Just like Jesus. The Spirit himself is truth.

→ The Spirit dwells in us and with us, as a helper. The Greek word for Helper is *Parakleton*. This word also means advocate, comforter, or advisor.

The Spirit is our trusted advisor, interceding for us in Christ, but also advising and guiding us in our daily walk. The Spirit's work is not complete at our baptism. We are not orphaned, the passage tells us. We are dearly loved, adopted children of God. How many of us long to see Jesus? Well, Christ has told us that He has left us something "better!"

See John 16:7 for this little nugget.

Nevertheless, I tell you the truth: it is to your advantage that I go away, for if I do not go away, the Helper will not come to you. But if I go, I will send him to you.

A little farther on in John 14:25-26, Jesus tells us again the work of the Spirit in our daily lives…He is our teacher. Look up these verses and note the work of the Spirit in the passage.

The Spirit, the often-quiet member of the Trinity, is at work in you! Every day! We do nothing outside of Him. We understand nothing outside of His work in us. What a blessing to have Truth not only spoken by God the Father, but come to Earth in Jesus Christ, and now *living in us*. The Spirit of Truth is constantly and completely available to us, working in us at all times and in all places.

And we carry the very truth the world desperately needs to see. But that's a discussion we'll save for tomorrow. For now, rejoice and rest in the Spirit of Truth, who rests deep inside of you.

<u>Exploration</u>
Read John 16:13. What authority does the Spirit speak in?

Share a time or a Scripture passage when the Spirit has guided you in Truth.

Day 4
The world really does care about Truth

Say what?! Because the people around me don't really seem to care. Sometimes when we try to share the Love of Jesus with someone, they seem completely shut off to it. Sometimes it seems as though people would rather sit in sin and darkness than be attuned to the light of truth. It is difficult to watch the news and see what seems like the blatant and utter disregard for God's truth- babies torn from the womb, marriage twisted and contorted, worshipping the created rather than the loving Creator. But frankly, when I see these things, do you know what I think God sees, why the end hasn't come and our time on this little planet is still impossibly necessary? Because out there is a hurting world, searching frantically for the Truth....*whether they know it or not.*

We have it, my friend. We have the truth. We hold it in our hands in the Scriptures; we hold it in our heart through the Spirit. Let us share it. Let us share it with compassion, and with joy, and with absolute resolute Truth.

One of the most famous conversations in Scriptures is about Truth. In fact, it's about a worldly man searching for truth.

Let's take a peek into John 18:33-38. Would you look that up for me?

Ugh. How I wish Scripture would have recorded an answer from Jesus! "What is truth?" At some point we all sit with that question. There are a million tiny little questions in that huge one- "What matters? What do I focus on? Where do I go from here? What is the point of it all?"

Christ's gentle, matter of fact questions and responses to Pilate can show us so much about the conversations we need to be having with those around us:

- Christ first *invites Pilate to a conversation*, rather than simply giving a response. How often would sharing Christ with someone work better if we asked more questions first. We don't need to have all the answers to share Jesus' love and truth and peace. We simply need to be willing to begin a conversation.
- Don't miss Jesus' words in verse 37 – indeed His entire purpose for coming to the world is found here - *to bear witness to the truth.* In this, as followers, as imitators or "little Christs", we simply bear witness to Him. His purpose is our purpose – *to bear witness to the truth*.
- Recognize that *Pilate is just not there yet*. The Spirit has not brought him to that place of understanding in which he realizes the answer to his question is standing right in front of him. Truth = Jesus. We will experience watching the backside of someone walk out the door; it isn't that they aren't searching for truth. It's just that they are not there yet, and that's ok for now. God is still writing the story.

Invite to the conversation, bear witness to the truth in our own redemptive story, and let the Spirit do His work.

Let's praise Him today for being invited to meet Him, with
overflowing Grace and Mercy.
Let's praise Him for the witness of so many.
Let's praise Him for the Spirit's work in my life.
He is so faithful.
He is so true.

Exploration
What do you suppose Pilate means by "What is truth?"

Why isn't a response from Jesus recorded in Scripture? Do you
think He responded at all or no?

Day 5
We can speak Truth to a hurting world

Bearing witness to a hurting world,
    Of who God is.
    Of what God does.
    Of His great plans.
    Of the Truth in Jesus Christ.
    Of a broken life, redeemed and set free.

The question comes- how in the world is He gonna use little ol' me to do all of that? The reality is, most of the time, he's going to use *words*. Obviously our actions matter, but it's the primary way He created us to communicate. He speaks to us in His Word. We share that Word with others through our words.

Let's open the Word to 2 Corinthians 6:3-11. Highlight or write in the margins here any phrases that stick out to you.

It would be so easy to get wrapped up in the instruction of this verse. We are constantly striving for patience, to be pure, to be more knowledgeable. Our Christian walk often seems like trudging through the mud of our own tiny capacity for following through. We want to show genuine love, especially in the face of suffering and heartache (v. 5).

But these verses are a declaration of a life in Christ, not the striving to be better Christians. Verse 8 is inclusive – we are not imposters, we are not deceivers. We live with hearts wide open (v. 11).

Hearts wide open. This is the work of the Spirit. This is in the calling, the gathering, and the enlightening work of the Spirit of Truth, through the saving work of Jesus, who is True. It is spoken over us by a Father, who can only speak Truth.

We were once hurting. We were once in darkness, asking "What is truth?" Our hearts are wide open, aching for the world around us, pouring out love and compassion because we have been there. We know what it was like without Truth. We desperately want more for them. We want Truth for them too.

And so we share it. Speaking freely, hearts wide open. With truthful speech, with genuine love. Remember, sisters, Biblical Truth, is not like the truth of this world, it testifies to itself, it cannot be hidden. No argument is necessary- simply a heart open wide.

Dear Lord, we thank You and praise You that You ARE TRUTH! Father, speak Your Truth to us, again and again. Jesus, be Truth in us every day. Spirit, open wide our hearts to share who you are, to bear witness to Your life giving Grace.
In Jesus name we pray.

Exploration

What is the hardest thing for you to overcome in sharing Truth with someone?

Share a Truth you have learned in your faith walk.

honor

Philippians 4:8
Finally, brothers, whatever is true, whatever is honorable,
whatever is just, whatever is pure, whatever is lovely, whatever is
commendable, if there is any excellence, if there is anything
worthy of praise, think about these things.

week two

Honor

We are women of Honor
We are Honored by God
God is deserving of Honor
Others deserve Honor
Humility and Honor

heart verse

a verse to meditate on for the week, to post
somewhere, or to memorize:
*Because you are precious in my eyes, and
honored, and I love you, I give men in return for
you, peoples in exchange for your life.*
Isaiah 43:4

Day 1
We are women of Honor

I have a big mouth. It's no secret. I have worked really hard over the years to get it under control and I'm happy to say that age, and experience, have brought me to a slightly better place in keeping my foot out of my mouth. However, dignified is not my strong suit. I tend towards compassionate, but unfailingly honest.

So, 1 Timothy 3:8-11 and I never quite gelled. To be more honest, take a closer look at verse 11 and you'll see my problem:

> *Deacons likewise must be dignified, not double-tongued,* *not addicted to much wine, not greedy for dishonest gain. They must hold the mystery of the faith with a clear conscience. And let them also be tested first; then let them serve as deacons if they prove themselves blameless. Their wives likewise must be dignified, not slanderers, but sober-minded, faithful in all things.*

Alright, slandering I can stay away from. I can even be sober-minded most of the time, concerned about things eternal, things that matter; but dignified. Yikes. Most Sundays I'm working hard to simply keep it together, as it were.

Why does all this matter? Because in searching the Scriptures, there are many different words for honor, with various definitions. But the Greek word used in our Philippians 4:8 passage is semna, which can mean dignified, serious, weighty, or deeply respected because it has majesty, because it is worthy of awe. So there are some options. Deeply respected certainly helps us understand it more, particularly in the context of our churches. Do you know another woman of God in your community that is deeply respected, who you deeply honor? Do you even know someone who you hold with a little bit of awe or weight?

I do, and I pray you do too! What a blessing these women of influence are in our lives. God, in these verses in Timothy, invites all of us, each as women of Christ, to be semna, worthy of a bit of awe and honor. I don't doubt that you probably are to someone around you and you have no idea.

You see, *I'm not so sure I'm awe inspiring, but I know that the God working in me is.* Oh yes, He is! Whether it's in quiet words of Truth or compassion undaunted, or friendship extended, forgiveness proclaimed - God's light shining purposefully through us is always honorable, always worthy of awe, with more than a touch of majesty. Our semna is always Him, flowing through us.

The question is whether we want to tamp down the light, *not* whether it's there. Do we let Him use us? Do we leave an open space in our hearts where dignity and honor can reside or do we fill it with unforgiveness, distrust, and bitterness? Do we let Him have His way with the influence we can be, or do we wrap ourselves up, away from His people, to stay safe from hurt, to spare energy?

Girls, he wants to use us, and He will. His Grace and Mercy is not dependent on my participation. But praises to Him, who invites me to be just a little piece of His majesty, His awe, and certainly His honor, during my short time on this planet.

Heads held high, girls! Dignified. We've got work to do. Kingdom work.

Exploration

Do you have someone you know, a woman of influence and dignity, whose faithfulness inspires you? Write a little bit about her.

Who do you have influence over in your church and life?

How do you see God working in different places in your life to share His honor with others?

Day 2
We are Honored by God

Today's study begins with our heart verse for the week. I call them heart verses because I am not great at memory work, but there are messages God leaves us in Scripture that He writes on our heart, through the Spirit, and it's a great practice to strategically tuck them in our hearts for a later date. That is of infinite value, eternal value.

Let's dive in and read Isaiah 43:1-7 in our Bibles.

I was in a Bible study a couple of years ago where we had to count how many times the word *you* or *your* was used in these seven verses. Try it now, it's quite striking. How many did you get?

22 times! Yes, 22 times in these seven verses of Scripture, God tells us in a multitude of ways how valued we are. I know Faith is not simply all about me and it's important that we understand that. But when I found this passage of Scripture, my heart ached with God's truth, in a way I had not heard or understood it before. God loves me.

God honors me. God has called me, God has washed me. God has ransomed me. God gave Jesus in exchange for me. God says this all over Scripture, but this is the only place I have ever found that God simply says those three little words our hearts were made to long for – **I love you.**

Straight from the mouth of God, not wrapped up tightly in abstract theological ideas, but plain for me to see. My honor, all people's honor, the Church's honor, whatever is honorable, is held tightly by a God who loves.

Fun fact: The Hebrew for honor in this verse (Isaiah 43:4) has essentially the same definition as the Greek word we found in Philippians 4:8 and studied on day one –semna, meaning heavy, burdensome, weighty and/or important.

Exploration
Read Isaiah 43:23-25 How did Israel fail to honor God?

In what ways do we fail to honor God at times?

What is God's response? How does this relate to verses 1-7?

Day 3
God is deserving of Honor

Today we open to a passage of Scripture that deals with real people. All of Scripture is real stories, but these people- they are Technicolor real, like, keeping-it-real kind of real. I think as Christians, these passages are extremely helpful for us, because we feel a little less alone in the walk. We tend to picture so many others around us with their act completely together, while we doggie paddle through the Christian walk, unsightly and disheveled. Or we tell ourselves we've got it so much more together than everyone else around us. Either way we take our eyes off the one who is truly worthy of honor – God.

Let's take out our Bibles and read 2 Samuel 6:16-23.
In this passage, David and his men have just returned the Ark of the Covenant, the very presence of God among His people, back to Israel. I'm not sure we have anything in our current time to compare this to. We have the presence of God at all times through the Holy Spirit (praise the Lord!), but for the people then, God's presence resided in His house, through the Ark. They needed it, like they needed water to survive. You better believe David was dancing in the streets!

Michal, struggling with bitterness and a myriad of her own baggage, is appalled and embarrassed, and accuses David of dishonor. The problem was where she fixed her eyes. She defined David's honor by the eyes of those around them, the people of Israel, and more problematic, by her own definition of what she saw as honorable. David, fixes his eyes firmly on His God, and instructs his wife that what she sees as honorable, and what the world defines as honorable, is very different than God's definition of honor. God's definition of honor - that's what matters to David.

I don't know about you, but I want to be where David was - contemptible by the world any day, if it means honorable to God. And the beauty is, that God's presence doesn't depend on our response. When we mess up, when we seek the world's honor, He still firmly planted His home in our hearts through the Spirit. We experience forgiveness and renewal and try again. That, my friends, that is something worth dancing about.

Exploration
In what ways do you think we get wrapped up in how the world defines honor (what is good/right)?

What is your favorite part of the worship service?

Day 4
Others deserve Honor

We know the Christian walk isn't simply about ourselves. It's a community, created and sustained by God himself. It's all about us, and very little about me. The idea of honor, particularly in the Old Testament is a communal concept. Honor exists in relationship. It's not something you can give or get for yourself. God bestows it on us, we bestow it on others, but it's always between "one anothers." This basic facts tells us that it's meant to be shared.

How can we share honor with others, who should we share this with, how can we let them know that they are also honored by God, held in high esteem...wanted?
Let's focus in today on who we can give honor to, with whom we can share the honor we ourselves receive from God.

The short answer is – everyone! Each and every person deserves honor because they are a created child of God (see Isaiah 43:1-7 from Day 2).

Another answer all over the Bible is – those to whom the world does not naturally give it.

1 Samuel 2:1-8 outlines many of those to whom honor is overlooked, those to whom we can take extra care to bestow honor towards. Look for the mention of these in the passage as you read.

- the feeble v. 4
- the barren v. 5
- the newly born and the dying v. 6
- the poor v. 7
- the needy (whether physically needy or emotionally needy) v. 8

Who is in your life you can give honor to? What people in our churches often feel left out?

How can we be a voice for the voiceless and bestow honor on the tiniest of people to the oldest and frailest?

Exploration
Pick one of the people groups from the 1 Samuel 2:1-8 and discuss how you, your family, or the church could reach out to honor them.

Write a prayer here about the people you identified above.

Day 5
Humility and Honor

In recent months my husband and I found ourselves locked in struggle, praying for humility for one of our precious children. When I prayed, asking God to give our son the gift of humility, I would always add the addendum, "and please be gentle…" Humility is a tough lesson. No one wants to learn it the hard way, but sometimes those lessons stick a bit better and we all know it.

In Luke 14:7-11, Jesus gives us a parable that teaches us more than a little about honor and humility. Read Luke 14:7-11,

> *Now he told a parable to those who were invited, when he noticed how they chose the places of honor, saying to them, "When you are invited by someone to a wedding feast, do not sit down in a place of honor, lest someone more distinguished than you be invited by him, and he who invited you both will come and say to you, 'Give your place to this person,' and then you will begin with shame to take the lowest place. But when you are invited, go and sit in the lowest place, so that when your host comes he may say to you, 'Friend, move up higher.' Then you will be honored in the presence of all who sit at table with you. For everyone who exalts himself will be humbled, and he who humbles himself will be exalted.*

Interesting fact: In the Gospels, honor is often related to festivities, parties, and banquets. It is often about our comparison of honor. How often do you compare yourself to others? This world of comparison, I think, is often magnified at weddings or parties. We want to be special to the host, to matter, to be included.

Does your honor come from the seat you are given in other people's lives or is it firmly rooted in having an honorable God dwelling in you?

Can you see the problem that might come with comparison? There will always be someone "more", someone "better" than us. But when we lose the comparison, when we understand that someone's specialness does not diminish our own specialness in God's eyes, we can live free of that "honor baggage." Free to live and serve and party at the banquet, instead of looking for the best seat.

Proverbs tells us not once but twice that humility comes before honor. (Proverbs 15:33, 18:12) We can see that Biblically, honor and humility have an intimate relationship, even though the world defines them as polar opposites. They go together like peas and carrots, macaroni and cheese. Isn't that just like God, confounding the world's wisdom?

In Esther 6, Haman, the archenemy of the Jewish captives in Babylon, is obsessed with honor. In your Bible, note how often the phrase "the man whom the king delights to honor" is stated. Seriously, Haman had an honor issue. If any of you have read Esther recently, you know that it doesn't go well for Haman. Chapter 6 is the beginning of Haman's downfall.

Here is the thing: we know the man the king delights to honor. His name is Jesus. Poor Haman. He didn't. He looked all over to get honor for himself. Mordecai was a threat to him, because he endlessly compared his honor with that received by others.

The King delights to honor you, girls. He honored you when He bowed His head and died to save and forgive you. We need not a single comparison in our life. We have Christ. And His honor looks a lot more like humility than we bargained for.

Thank you, Jesus, for loving me and teaching me humility in Your life and death on Earth. Let my honor be in Your death and resurrection, in being Your precious child, bought at a price. Let me share that humility and honor with those around me. Bring me to Your final banquet, where we will rejoice together for eternity. In Christ, Amen.

HEIDI GOEHMANN

week three

Just

Jesus is Justice
Justice is salvation
Justice in our daily walk
Justice at last!
When Justice does equal fairness

heart verse

a verse to meditate on for the week, to post
somewhere, or to memorize:

*...for all have sinned and fall short of the
glory of God, and all are justified freely by
his grace...*

Romans 3:23-24a (NIV)

Day 1
Jesus is Justice

Justice is important to us. Middle schoolers go through a developmental phase, according to Erik Erickson, called Identity v. Role Confusion. During this phase they start to identify what is important to them and begin the struggle of trying to see life from other people's perspectives. Justice is a huge part of this development phase. The middle schoolers in your life probably wants to be assured that everything, absolutely everything is fair. They are deeply disturbed by the hurtful things other people say and do, mainly because they do not understand how the world can be so unjust. They wonder what did they do to deserve hurtful words, harsh actions from their friends and school mates.

At some point adolescents move on to other developmental phases. They do this through loving individuals in their lives, helping them come to terms with the fact that life is just not fair. Life will not be fair this side of heaven. In reality, we all continue to struggle with justice to some degree, in our lives. How can the murderer be spared and the young mother overcome by cancer? Why does it feel like evil prevails? If God was just – wouldn't He have come to fix everything already?

One of my favorite songs talks about the fact that grace in its truest sense makes life not fair. (Relient K - Be My Escape) The lyrics to this song always stick out to me, because our concept of grace is so tainted by our life on planet Earth.

We have a God who is fully Just and fully Gracious. Life around us does not represent God well. It never will. Life will fail us. God will not. So when we are looking for justice, know that we can only find it in the One who is Justice itself.
Let's find the proof! Read Acts 3:14-16 in your Bibles. For the full story, read Acts 3:1-16, it's beautiful and worth the extra effort.

In verse 14, The Righteous One can also be translated the Just One. The Greek word here is Dikaion, which shares the same root as "just" or "right" in our Philippians 4:8 passage – dikaios. So Biblically speaking, if we are looking for what is just, or what justice is, Acts 3:14-16 tells us the answer is Jesus. Jesus is justice. Jesus is righteousness. Read verse 16 again... *"And his name—by faith in his name—has made this man strong whom you see and know, and the faith that is through Jesus has given the man this perfect health in the presence of you all."* And His name...His name of Justice, His name of Rightness -- makes us right with God. Grace makes life not fair. God is able to see us as right, because Jesus is Right. In His justice and rightness we have strength to deal with a life that is simply not fair.

This week we'll deal with a difficult topic, but know that it is all wrapped up in the name of Jesus. Once again, He is the answer, the definition, the everything. Let's praise God for a "not fair" life, full of grace, and one another to share it with.

Exploration

When you were an adolescent what questions do you remember asking and struggling with?

What things about life seem "not fair" around you?

Day 2
Justice is salvation

On day one, we talked about how difficult justice and fairness are to wrestle with. Today, we're going to address justice from a different perspective. Maybe it will keep us motivated to discover more. More Bible, more God, more Jesus.

Today, the fact in front of us is that we NEED justice.

As far as God goes, we often think that Grace frees us from justice. From this perspective the tone of justice seems a bit more sinister, a little bit evil. We slide into thinking that justice and grace are diametrically opposite. But the Bible tells us that Justice is full of Grace and Grace is full of Justice. They are woven together in God's perfect tapestry of relationship with His people, with us, His precious children.

Let's read Romans 3:21-26 to get something solid under our feet in this discussion (focus in on v. 26):

> *But now the righteousness of God has been manifested apart from the law, although the Law and the Prophets bear witness to it—the righteousness of God through faith in Jesus Christ for all who believe. For there is no distinction: for all have sinned and fall short of the glory of God, and are justified by his grace as a gift, through the*

redemption that is in Christ Jesus, whom God put forward as a propitiation by his blood, to be received by faith. This was to show God's righteousness, because in his divine forbearance he had passed over former sins. It was to show his righteousness at the present time, so that he might be just and the justifier of the one who has faith in Jesus.

Now – the Greek for the word righteousness and justice in this passage, again have the same root word...our word for "just" in Philippians, *dikaios*. To clarify, go back and read the passage above one more time and use the word justice, when you see the word "righteousness." You'll find 7 instances where the same root word is utilized. This passage shows us Justice and Jesus are wrapped up and tied together like the cords of a rope. The cords of a rope thrown to us, to save our life.

Jesus is Justice and He is the justifier.

- All have sinned. Adam and Eve sinned in the Garden. You and I sin every day.
- Justice demands our death. God's right and perfect justice, which we cannot argue with. He is God, we are not.
- ***Christ's act of mercy, act of complete Grace in His death on the cross and resurrection from the tomb brings us a New Justice that we call Salvation.***

This is why we call it Justification, friends. Justice and Grace all wrapped up and tied together.

How does this make a difference in our life? First, God Is so much more vast and large and deep than we make Him. He does not think like we think. He does not act like we would act. He is God and when the world is pushing in and we can't understand where and when justice will come from, we at least have a basic answer – Jesus. We look for that day when Jesus comes back and everything is 100% right and just and true. (More on this on day four!)

Second, when we want justice, we can understand that in God's economy it looks like Grace. When the high school shooter intrudes into our lives, when evil rears it's ugly head into our homes and our families, we know our response - Grace. The two are not separate but wrapped together in the person of Jesus, and so shall they be in our lives. We can offer Grace, we can search for moments of Grace, when others cry out for vengeance, because we ourselves have received the same.

Day 3
Justice in our daily walk

On day 2, we talked about Justice and Grace being wrapped up together. What does that look like in our lives, though? How do Justice and Grace flow together in our interactions with those around us?

Understanding that the two can't be neatly separated helps us to identify incongruence in our faith walk- when things don't quite line up in the way we live and the beliefs we hold firmly.

We cannot have Justice without Grace. It's the basic principle of no Law without Gospel, no Gospel without Law.

What is incongruence? When we want the God of Love, but don't want Him to judge our choices. We live a life of "whatever, God loves me anyway!" and ignore that God hates sinful and destructive behavior that separates us from Him. When we live believing that every affliction and struggle is God punishing us. That God rains down Justice when we're bad, and Love and Grace when we're good. When we try to live a life "right" and "perfect" with God, so that we can have control of our life and our plans will prevail.

When we create a picture of justice that fits what we want, ignoring what God may want.

Romans seems to have a lot about Justice! Let's turn to Romans 12 for help on Justice/Grace living. Look this one up in your Bibles and note the last sentence in your margin here.

Verse 19 sums up Justice/Grace living perfectly. "Leave it." "On the contrary."

- It will not look like the rest of the world. It will not look "normal." So often when the world screams for justice, what they really want is vengeance, and our God tells us to leave it. To let the God of the universe work in His perfect Justice and Mercy and take care of the problem. Pray about it, girls. In prayer, God hears our cries. He acknowledges our struggle and we can trust in Him to act.
- It will almost always look contrary to what the world tells us to do. Trust the advice of people who read the Bible with you and share in the connected discussion of life around the Word. Do not trust the advice of the news media or Joe-Smo at work who tells you to repay evil for evil. When evil pushes itself into your life -- respond with Love, respond with Grace, respond "on the contrary."

Beloved, the Spirit is strong and able. He lives in us and acts in us to enable the impossible – Justice and Grace poured out together on a hurting world.

Father, thank you for your perfect Justice and perfect Love. You give us Hope when the world is crashing down. You will make everything right. We trust you, Lord. Help us when we struggle to trust. In Jesus precious name. Amen.

Day 4
Justice At last!

Sometimes we just need to know that there will be justice. We join with the Psalmist,

How long, Oh, Lord! How long…

The early Christians went through such ardent and constant persecution that they needed to know their labor was not in vain and the suffering would end. And so, St. Paul writes to them in 2 Thessalonians 1:3-8. Dig into your Bibles today with this passage.

Some exciting bullet points in this passage about justice –

- Persecution will be a part of our Christian walk – yuck, but true. And we found out in week one that Truth is better. ☺ Verse 7 tells us that relief will come.

- Verse 7 also tells us that we may not be afflicted, but others are. Have you seen the images of Christians across the world dying for their faith? We can pray this verse over those undergoing persecution. We can cry out for justice on their behalf, praying "Come, Lord Jesus, Come."

- There will be an end to the struggle and it will be Glorious. We can "leave it" to God, like we talked about in day 3, and then stand in awe one day when He comes "with mighty angels in flaming fire." What a picture! God sitting on the mercy seat carried on wheels of fire and holy angels (Daniel 7:9), at His name knees bowing, tongues confessing (Philippians 2:10-11). Wow!

Perhaps, most notably, this passage tells us that God cares. He is the God who sees. Our pain, our struggle does not go unnoticed. When evil pushes in, our Just and Gracious God will respond in His time. Often the problem is, we don't like the timing. But I think we're getting there. We need each other. Just like the Apostle Paul, we can spur one another on.

We can pray, praise, and give thanks with one another.
We can cry together in the unjust, and rejoice together as His plans unfold (v. 3).
We can boast at one another's faithfulness (v. 4).

We can verbally point out the evidence of faith we see in the believers around us (v. 5).

I can see the evidence, sister. I can see it in you, right now, as we share in the Word together. Thank you for sharing this moment with me. May He keep us faithful to the End.

Day 5
When Justice does equal fairness

We've been talking all we about the fact that we are given the opportunity to give Grace when others call for vengeance, but is there ever a time for Justice on this Earth? When fairness does matter and we should fight for it?

The Bible addresses justice in terms of fairness from the vantage point of our own walk, but not us applying it to the walk of others. So when we seek fairness, it should be in ourselves. We can give fairness as a gift to others. This sets us apart and is a work of the Holy Spirit and Faith in us.

In Luke 12:57-58, Jesus tells the Pharisees…

> *And why do you not judge for yourselves what is right? As you go with your accuser before the magistrate, make an effort to settle with him on the way, lest he drag you to the judge, and the judge hand you over to the officer, and the officer put you in prison.*

Jesus tells us that he trusts us to make a good case for ourselves and for our relationships. He tells us that we are capable. It reminds me of parenting with high expectations. It's encouraging to know that our God believes us capable of judging what is right and just and fair. He has fully equipped us!

Again, the Bible encourages Masters (or we'll go with Bosses in our current context) to be just, or fair in Colossians 4:1...

> *Masters, treat your bondservants justly and fairly, knowing that you also have a Master in heaven.*

Titus 1:8 pops up again....

> *For an overseer, as God's steward, must be above reproach. He must not be arrogant or quick-tempered or a drunkard or violent or greedy for gain, but hospitable, a lover of good, self-controlled, upright, holy, and disciplined.*

We saw that verse last week when we were talking about an overseer, or someone who is a leader being honorable (*semna*). The word for upright in the ESV has that same root we've seen all week – diakos. A Christian leader is exhorted to lead with justice, with fairness.

And lastly, Ephesians 6:1, exhorts the youngest followers....

> *Children, obey your parents in the Lord, for this is right.*

God doesn't leave us in the lurch when seeking answers for our daily lives. He gives us bread for each day, wisdom for each situation, grace for each moment.

Thank you, Father! You are full of so many good things. Help Justice to reign in our lives. Help us to live in Justice/Grace Living, through Your Spirit. We thank and praise You for all that You are, all that You have done, and all You continue to do. In Jesus's name. Amen.

Exploration

Where in your life can you extol fairness to those around you?

pure

week four

Pure

Pure Redemption
Pure Hearts
Pure Minds
Pure Relationships
Pure Lives

heart verse

a verse to meditate on for the week, to post
somewhere, or to memorize:

*All who have this hope in him purify
themselves, just as he is pure.*
1 John 3:3 (NIV)

Day 1
Pure redemption

My friend once told me she was going to buy me a shirt that says "I love Jesus, but I cuss a little."

It's true. I don't actually cuss much, but I'm not sure I'd qualify for the Christian purity award. Good thing there's no such thing. My past was rocky, my present more like bumpy, and my future is firmly in His grip.

The Greek word for pure in Philippians 4:8, is *hagna*. In looking up its definition, I was bombarded by words like innocent, free from sin, modest, holy, sacred, without spoil. These are strong words. The guilt was overwhelming. Free from sin, hardly. Uncontaminated – I laugh. There is a reason I only stay in touch with a few very close friends from high school. Who wants to relive those days?

Hagna is an adjective, it describes something, but in 1 John 1:5-10 we can also find purity as a verb, as an action, and of course it is a work of Jesus Christ, not me.

> *This is the message we have heard from him and proclaim to you, that God is light, and in him is no darkness at all. If we say we have fellowship with him while we walk in darkness, we lie and do not practice the truth. But if we*

*walk in the light, as he is in the light, we have fellowship
with one another, and the blood of Jesus his Son cleanses
us from all sin. If we say we have no sin, we deceive
ourselves, and the truth is not in us. If we confess our sins,
he is faithful and just to forgive us our sins and to cleanse
us from all unrighteousness.*

Girls, darkness is miserable and scary, but it is not us. Christ is in
us. Christ cleanses us. The phrase to cleanse is also translated to
make pure, or better yet- to remove all filth. This is the work of
Christ. Darkness is the shame that no longer has a place in our
lives. We are light women, light people. No matter our look of
purity, our feeling of purity of the past or present, He declares us
purely redeemed, Pure Ones to Him in our confession.

2 Corinthians 7:11 offers us an interesting take on repentance
and confession:

*See what this godly sorrow has produced in you: what
earnestness, what eagerness to clear yourselves, what
indignation, what alarm, what longing, what concern,
what readiness to see justice done. At every point you have
proved yourselves to be innocent in this matter.*

In Corinthians we are told that innocence (purity) is a fruit of
repentance, not a result of perfect behavior.

*"See what this godly sorrow has produced in
you...you have proved yourselves to be innocent..."*

Of course we need to stay away from the things that invite sin
into our lives. Yes, yes, and yes! But more importantly we are
invited to stand on the road as a God who runs with open arms
to embrace us and let Purity itself overwhelm us with Mercy and
Grace.

Exploration

When have you doubted your purity?

When have you judged others based on their outward actions as pure or impure?

What is your current practice of confession, asking God for forgiveness of your sins and acknowledging the grace He offers (when, where, how often)? (No guilt! Only Grace!)

Day 2
Pure hearts

I can not talk about purity without the song "Give Us Clean Hands" popping into my head. While reading through verses for this study, I studiously ignored the singspiration going on in my head, until low and behold – there was the song in my Bible. Sometimes, I think, when we're singing a hymn or song, we think, "Gee, these are really nice lyrics." When so often, they're so nice, because the Ancient of Days wrote them in His Bible and on our hearts long ago.

These words can be found in Psalm 24. Let's look up that psalm. Write verse 4 below.

In any given Bible translation the phrase "pure heart" is mentioned roughly 9 times throughout Scripture. It is a topic in both the Old and New Testaments; a topic of wisdom literature, the Psalms, the Gospels, and the Epistles. It's clearly an important element when we talk about purity.

What is a pure heart? How do we get one? Why does it matter?

Psalm 24 gives us a window – a pure heart does not lift up his soul to an idol. I lift up my soul to an idol when I make my will and my plans vital before God's. When I treat my husband with contempt or disrespect. When I under-appreciate the good gifts of a beautiful home and healthy children because it all seems like so much work on any given day. I lift up my soul to an idol when I want more stuff, better stuff. So far, I'm not doing so well on the pure heart front.

Psalm 51 gives us another window into what a pure heart is and where we can get it. Look it up in your Bible. It may look a little long, but I guarantee it's worth it! David shows us in this Psalm that God's forgiveness is free and freely given.

Both of these beautiful Psalms are written by David. Both wrestle with the real desire to be pure before God. To offer Him our absolute best. There is so much comfort for me in knowing that David lived the same sinner-saint life that I live today. I want to have a pure heart, to cast down idols and stand firm in Him, who is my Rock. And God says, "Yes!"

Let us be a generation that seeks His face and plants our feet firmly in His solid ground!

But in my dark moments, where all is revealed before Him, I know I am always going to fail. There will always be one more idol, lurking around the next corner, wooing me with false promises. If you look in your Bible, there is a small notation under the title of Psalm 51 stating,

> *To the choirmaster. A Psalm of David, when Nathan the prophet went to him, after he had gone in to Bathsheba.*

Yikes. David was so far from purity. Yet God in His Mercy, penned this Psalm, through him –

> ***Create in me a clean (a pure) heart, O God....***
>
> ***Renew a right Spirit within me....***

God renews, God purifies. God helps us to cast down idols at every turn in our lives. God grants us clean hands, pure hearts.

We are seeking His face together, girls! Thank you for sharing the journey with me.

Exploration

What is a pure heart and how do we get one?

What idols have you struggled with? Which idols do you see others around you struggling with?

How can we create conversation about God casting down our idols, whether it is in a public forum, like Facebook or a meeting, or in private conversation?

Day 3

Pure Minds

It is helpful that Scripture addresses purity from many facets. It brings to mind the verse tucked in Luke 10 -

> And he answered, "You shall love the Lord your God with all your heart and with all your soul and with all your strength and with all your mind, and your neighbor as yourself." (v. 27)

Jesus Himself recognizes here that we are multi-faceted people, and each of these areas needs to be addressed in our lives. We can see His law, as well as our failure, in each area also – when our hearts are hard, or our strength fails, or our minds are filled with doubt and words of hurtfulness – but we can also see His Grace clearly:

He restores our souls (Psalm 23:3)

He heals the brokenhearted and binds up their wounds (Psalm 147:3)

He is strong when we are weak (2 Corinthians 12:10)

He gives us a sound mind (2 Timothy 1:7)

So with that firmly established, let's delve into a great verse that establishes for us what pure minds look like.

James 3:17-
> *But the wisdom from above is first pure, then peaceable, gentle, open to reason, full of mercy and good fruits, impartial and sincere.*

Wisdom in this verse is our intelligence and our skills - things that are seated in our mind. What does this verse teach about what pure is? Consider the questions with each point and write some notes in the margins on each.

- Pure... well, there's our word! Holy, of God, especially in worship, according to the Greek. God's Word, always guaranteed pure and holy. How can we keep it pure in our lives?

- Peaceable, peace loving, peace seeking...how can we be peace seeking with what we learn, and discuss, and post online?

- Gentle...how can we be gentle with our minds? How is wisdom gentle? When is it not gentle and how is that problematic?

- Open to reason....does that sound like our lives on Facebook? In our conversations and discussion? Are we open to wisdom? How do we help those around us to be open to wisdom when we are trying to share from the Word?

- Full of mercy and good fruits...does the wisdom we think, speak, or receive contain mercy? God's wisdom, through His Word and others, always contains mercy.

- Impartial... How can we keep our wisdom impartial? Impartiality and avoiding favoritism in our families, at work, and in our lives is His Spirit in us.

- Sincere...this has to do with authenticity, does our walk match our talk? Do we let God's light flow or squelch it to blend in with the culture? Are we sincere with those around us, avoiding gossip and double talk?

Yikes! That's a lot to take in, and a lot to watch out for in our lives. Sisters, do not feel the weight of being "not enough." Not good enough, not smart enough, not authentic enough. That is not the message of this text. Nor is it ever the message of Scripture. This passage simply tells us what God's wisdom looks like. He is perfectly perfect and that is what works in us. The sanctified life is a challenge for sure, a journey of imperfection, but it is also the experience of grace and mercy.

The purified life is purified once and for all by Jesus Christ, and then daily by His Spirit working in us and through His people. We have the gift of His Word. When in doubt, He does not keep His wisdom from us, but reveals it plainly. He is our wisdom. He is our purity.

Dear Lord, we pray that you would keep our hearts, souls, minds, and strength firmly fixed on You. Give us pure minds, give us pure hearts through Your good and gracious gifts. In Jesus name, Amen.

Exploration

Look up 2 Corinthians 11:1-15, especially verses 2-4. How do pure doctrine and pure minds intersect?

Day 4
Pure Relationships

First, you must know that I have a very strong opinion that Faith is a battle won in community, and as a transference of this fact, marriage can only be done well *in community*. We need one another. This is what the mission of life together is all about. We were created by a relational God to share His love relationally. That may be inside our marriages and families, but it is also as support from one another in those very things.

When we look at the next passage, let's think on that - how these verses apply to our relationships, how they apply to life together, beyond our homelife. Jot down words that address these subjects on your page here.
Let's read 1 Peter 3:1-7.

At first glance, these look like terribly stick-in-your-crawl, law-oriented verses. Yikes, there is about 50 things I need to work on in my life and about 2 for the men in my life, including taking care of me as the "weaker vessel." Um…

Many of you do not know me well, but these kinds of verses can be challenging for recovering feminists, such as myself. But let's set aside all the theologically difficult thoughts swirling, and settle on one aspect of these verses, pertinent to our study - what is Pure.

I think this verse is primarily about how we respond in relationship.

> *"...they may be won without a word...*
> *when they see your respectful and pure conduct."*

Clearly, the verse is talking about wives responding to their husbands, but what other relationships do you have that build up or tear down depending on your response? Remember that this involves messing up and forgiving more often than it does perfect living. Purity of conduct is not perfect conduct. Holiness is authenticity of Faith in life. Fruits of the Spirit poured out because Christ is welling up. *Forgiveness* is what purity in our lives and in our marriages look like.

Forgiveness equals pure relationships.

Exploration

How can we build up our family relationships and friendships through forgiveness?

How can we build up the marriages around us, not just our own, or even as single people through forgiveness in our own lives?

Day 5
Pure Lives

Today we tackle a difficult passage that draws a line in the sand between Christians and non-Christians. It's the kind of passage that you wouldn't use to share the Gospel with anyone, but it's essential for us to be able to share the Gospel with anyone.

Titus 1:15-16

> *To the pure, all things are pure, but to the defiled and unbelieving, nothing is pure; but both their minds and their consciences are defiled. They profess to know God, but they deny him by their works. They are detestable, disobedient, unfit for any good work.*

We could read these verses with a whole lot of spitfire and disdain – words like defiled and detestable jump out. They are strong words and so they come to the forefront of our minds when we internalize the passage.

Let's read the passage again with compassion rolling off our tongues.

- Belief is a huge commitment. We avoid this talk because we do not want to introduce any theology of glory into the picture. Committing is certainly a work of the Spirit, something we are unable to do on our own. However, look at the huge elephant in the passage – belief changes everything. And my friends, I think there are a whole lot of people that are simply not ready for that kind of commitment. We can have compassion when we share the message of Jesus, because we are sharing something huge and life changing. Something that might need a "moment" if you will, to sit, and brew, and blossom.

- Purity is a language for believers. We get so frustrated with the world around us. We see sexual sin abounding and destroying young lives and hearts, we watch as the world twists His Word to suit their purposes, we shudder at the defilement of children, and babies tossed aside in a world that devalues and devalues and devalues some more. As believers we get trapped in sin, certainly, but we should not be surprised by the impurity of the world around us. It is frustrating and worth confronting, but with compassion on our lips and in our hearts-

They do not know.

They do not know as we know.

They do not know the One who is Pure, the One who is Holy, the one who changes everything.

Unbelief matters. This is why, friend or family member, we are desperate to tell you the message of Jesus Christ. He changes absolutely everything. Everything. Our belief makes us look different to the world. It will attract some. It will annoy others. But it will be pure, because He is pure. It will involve confession and forgiveness, authenticity and transparency, a heart broken, but a heart fully restored, made Holy and Pure.

Sisters, I leave you with our heart verse for the week, wrapped up in a broader passage about God's love, our special place as His children, and things yet to come.
1 John 3:1-3:

> *See what kind of love the Father has given to us, that we should be called children of God; and so we are. The reason why the world does not know us is that it did not know him. Beloved, we are God's children now, and what we will be has not yet appeared; but we know that when he appears we shall be like him, because we shall see him as he is. And everyone who thus hopes in him purifies himself as he is pure.*

We shall see Him as He is. Meanwhile, His Hope in us, lavished and poured out on a hurting world - that is Purity.

Exploration

Who in your life can you pray for today? Who can you share with and pray these prayers with?

Who could use an extra dose of compassion because of the sin of the world pushing in?

Philippians 4:8
Finally, brothers, whatever is true, whatever is honorable,
whatever is just, whatever is pure, whatever is lovely, whatever is
commendable, if there is any excellence, if there is anything
worthy of praise, think about these things.

week five

Lovely

A Lovely, relationship God
Friendship is Lovely
Where He is, is Lovely
We are Lovely to God
Celebrating is Lovely

heart verse

a verse to meditate on for the week, to post
somewhere, or to memorize:

*How lovely is your dwelling place, O LORD of
hosts!*

Psalm 84:1

Day 1
A Lovely, relationship God

From the moment I decided to work through this Scripture in Philippians, I was intrigued by the inclusion of the word lovely.

First of all, let it roll off your tongue – Lovely...

Isn't it pretty? Isn't the word itself kind of soft or milky?

It's not a word we overuse in our culture. Which is refreshing in itself. It has the same kind of lilt as words like grace, and mercy. It is much less intimidating than words like justice and excellence. It is very simply, lovely.

The Greek is even more intriguing. It's like the creamy caramel center to the milky chocolate outer shell.

The Greek word for lovely, in Philippians 4:8, only ever occurs in Scripture in this passage. But the theme of it, I think you will see is all over Scripture. So what's the word?

Prosphile – pleasing, acceptable, agreeable, and grateful.

Not horribly unique, but let's look at the two roots to this single word. Pros, which means extending toward, and phileo. Does that ring a bell with anyone? Phileo is affectionate caring. Phileo is the Greek word used to express friendship love. It's perhaps most famous from John 21:15-19 as Jesus questions Peter about his affection for Him carried out in the work of the kingdom. (Feel free to check this passage out, especially using the biblehub.com's interlinear tool to see the difference in the Greek words.)

So what good does all this "neat" and "kind of cool" Greek language knowledge do for us? The place of lovely in the Philippians 4 passage, I think gives us a little more insight into who our Great God is. And that, my friends, is....relational.

Scripture shows us time and again that relationship matters more to God than anything - our relationship with Him, the relationships of His people, and relationships or relating to others, to share His love with the world.

God loves us. Lovely, love. Wait a minute! Lovely is not an accidental word. This is a purposeful word, with a purposeful place in Scripture and in our hearts. It is knit together and chosen by God for our understanding.

God's love speaks volumes into our lives and into the lives of those around us. One commentator's translation* of *prosphile* is "worth the effort to have and embrace." You are worth the effort to God. There is a physical affection attached to our relationship with Him and our relationship with others, through Him. He longs to pour His affection on you through His Word, His sacraments, and His people. Others long to be shown an affectionate and loving God through affectionate and loving people.

Relationships are hard. They take energy. They take effort, a whole lot of it. But we can be assured of one more thing through Scripture....

Relationships, they really are lovely.

<u>Exploration</u>

How does God's love poured into you help you put energy into other relationships?

In what ways do you most clearly hear and feel God's love for you (a certain Bible verse, the means of grace, through a person or action, etc.)?

Day 2
Friendship is Lovely

Tucked inside of all the wisdom found in John's Gospel, we find a section of verses that offer us another sandwich. Not the lunch kind of sandwich, but the relationship kind of sandwich. Remember in week one of our study when we had a grace and truth sandwich in John 1? Jesus full of grace and truth and coming from grace and truth?

John is evidentially a big fan of chiastic structure, or emphasizing his point with "the sandwich."

Let's read John 15:12-17 in our Bibles.

Underline or highlight in your Bible the word "friends" in one color and the words "love" or "loved" in another. First, can you see the sandwich? This is my commandment – love one another (v. 12). These things I command you – love one another (v. 17).

What is the meat of the sandwich this time? *Friendship.*

Jesus calls us His friends. He pours His agape love into us in many ways, as children, as fellow heirs and brothers and sisters, as His Bride. Let us not forget, He calls us friend. Highlight the lines in the hymn below that are speaking to you today.

What a *friend* we have in Jesus,
All our sins and griefs to bear!
What a privilege to carry
Ev'rything to God in prayer!
Oh, what peace we often forfeit;
Oh, what needless pain we bear--
All because we do not carry
Ev'rything to God in prayer!

Have we trials and temptations?
Is there trouble anywhere?
We should never be discouraged--
Take it to the Lord in prayer.
Can we find a *Friend* so faithful
Who will all our sorrows share?
Jesus knows our ev'ry weakness--
Take it to the Lord in prayer.

Are we weak and heavy-laden,
Cumbered with a load of care?
Precious Savior, still our refuge--
Take it to the Lord in prayer.
Do thy *friends* despise, forsake thee?
Take it to the Lord in prayer.
In His arms He'll take and shield thee,
Thou wilt find a solace there.

Joseph M. Scriven (What a Friend We Have in Jesus - public domain)

God exists in friendship. There is a reason friendship is such a precious thing, especially to us lady-folk. We may not need a boatload of friends, but we all need one or two really good friends. We were made to long for that friend, as a way to see Christ's love alive and active in our lives.

Need a friend? You have one in Jesus. A real man, who walked the real and difficult soil of Earth. But it's ok to long for a today friend, a right in front of you drinking your coffee friend, a hug you when it hurts kind of friend, a laugh until you cry kind of friend. That's Jesus too. Poured from one heart to another, and this is a precious offering of ourselves to Him, in friendship with one another.

How many times is prayer mentioned in the hymn above? It's not a coincidence. God is listening. Pray for a friend. Thank Him for a friend. Embrace Him as your very best friend, who never ever fails, when everyone else does.

Lovely.

Exploration

What do you need or desire in a friend?

What aspects of God have you learned in friendship?

How is Jesus the perfect friend?

Day 3
Where He is, is Lovely

Let's start today with Psalm 84. Check it out in your Bible.

Well, that just kind of gets you going, right? What a happy psalm, a bright psalm, uplifting. It strikes me how many exclamation marks are in this Psalm. Although not in the original Hebrew, it was clear to many a translator that this Psalm screams exclamation point!

And why? Because we have a God who gives us a dwelling place with Him. Since the Garden of Eden, we were created to dwell with God. For the Hebrew people of the Old Testament, the tabernacle, and then the Temple was to them the place where they could, without a doubt, be in the presence of the One, True Living God. The Psalm expresses their longing for it. That one day with God is better than thousands anywhere else. That ours heart and flesh cry to be with the Living God.

Then, God sent Jesus. The Living God to dwell with His people on the Earth, to die on the cross, and rise again in New Life for our forgiveness and salvation. Then, God created churches and sanctuaries. We, like the Old Testament psalmist, long for fellowship and worship together, to draw together, to study His Word and share His sweet communion.

But, just so we're clear – where does God dwell? Not in buildings made by man - **He dwells in people.** This is something that is vital for us to remember. We can build pretty buildings and throw money at nice sanctuaries, but without the people, it is not God.

John 14:15-17 tells us:

> *If you love me, you will keep my commandments. And I will ask the Father, and he will give you another Helper, to be with you forever, even the Spirit of truth, whom the world cannot receive, because it neither sees him nor knows him. You know him, for he dwells with you and will be in you.*

God is where people filled with His Spirit are. You are a living, breathing, walking dwelling place for the True and Living God. He fills Your heart and it overflows onto those around you. People longing for His presence will see it, not in a building, but in you.

This is one reason why people so rarely just walk in churches, when they are looking for the Lord. Somewhere deep in us, God knit an internal GPS system to seek Him through one another.

This means loveliness is in each of us and this is where others will find what is lovely. When we look at our neighbor, believer or unbeliever, we can see a place God's image dwells, and God's Spirit can fill. Who around you has a need, an empty place, ready for His Spirit to fill?

Our neighbor, His dwelling place. Precious to Him. Worth the effort.

Day 4
We are Lovely to God

The word lovely, always brings to mind one face for me, my 13-year old daughter, Macee. There is just something about her that is so lovely. Some people are dignified, some people exude creativity, Macee, she reflects what is lovely in her face, her spirit, and her gentle heart. Do you have anyone who reflects loveliness in your life?

When God sees us, He sees lovely. He knit each of us together and crafted us carefully. We are not random chances of an evolutionary process, but made with care by a real Creator, who molds us with His hands out of the dust. He shapes our DNA, our bone structure, and numbers the hairs on our head.

The word lovely is found most often in the Bible in the Song of Songs (or Song of Solomon, depending on your translation). This makes sense, knowing the context of the book is in the courtship and marriage relationship of two people, as well as the greater image of Christ and His Bride the Church. All of that, in itself, is lovely.

The Song of Songs is so very expressive. It details each lover's beauty, and the beauty and purity of the marriage relationship. It's intimidating, and sensual, but worth the time. Today, I'd like to dive into 4 verses within the Song that capture aspects of our physical selves that God expresses are lovely to Him. Is our soul lovely to Him? Of course, it is of the utmost value to Him. Is our heart lovely to Him? Yes. God sees our whole selves as His precious creation. But sometimes we forget that our physical form was made lovely by Him, and even with sin in the world and deformities, disease, and abuse, He sees our face, our hands, our hair, our hips, all of it, as lovely.

Let's open it up and see what He has to say. With each verse, consider what feature is being called lovely. I'll throw in Heidi's Brief Commentary after each verse to give you my thoughts on it.

Song of Songs 1:5:

> *(She) I am very dark, but lovely,*
>
> > *O daughters of Jerusalem, like the tents of Kedar,*
>
> *like the curtains of Solomon.*

Our skin is lovely. All skin is lovely. God created a myriad of colors in His people. He molded our DNA to allow for diversity which is a blessing.

Song of Songs 1:10:

> *Your cheeks are lovely with ornaments,*
>
> *your neck with strings of jewels.*

Our cheeks, our necks are lovely. These are not body parts we look in the mirror and think, "Wow, I have a great neck." But God does! I think our cheeks are best on display when we smile...coincidence? I think not.

Song of Songs 2:14:

> *O my dove, in the clefts of the rock,*
>
> > *in the crannies of the cliff, let me see your face,*
>
> > *let me hear your voice, for your voice is sweet,*

and your face is lovely.

Our face, our voice is lovely to God. Imagine the joy He feels when we speak of Him with our lips. When we praise Him, or cry out to Him with our voice. He gave us that voice. He crafted our faces.

Song of Songs 4:3:

Your lips are like a scarlet thread,

and your mouth is lovely.

Your cheeks are like halves of a pomegranate

behind your veil.

Our lips are lovely to God. He made them for speaking words of encouragement, for kissing our husbands, and for tasting His bountiful harvest and sweet communion.

Song of Songs 6:4:

(He) You are beautiful as Tirzah, my love,

lovely as Jerusalem,

awesome as an army with banners.

All of us. We are lovely to Him. We are His army, standing strong in His Spirit, proclaiming His name to the nations.

We can take all of these verses symbolically and apply them to Christ and His Bride, the Church, but most commentators agree that it's also an individual story of love. Christ does love us as individuals, see us as individuals, and shape our hearts as individuals. I think we rob ourselves of His goodness when we do not see the love God is expressing for each of us in these verses.

I hope today, you feel filled with loveliness, because the Bible tells you so.

Much love, sisters. Much love.

Exploration

Who is lovely in your life?

What is your favorite feature God has gifted you with (on your body)?

How can we build up one another and particularly the young women around us, in regards to body image and God's lovely design?

Day 5
Celebrating is Lovely

Luke 15 gives us a different take on lovely. For our final day of discovering all things lovely let's reflect back on the root of lovely being in relationship, or more specifically, friendship.

Luke 15 is a chapter of Scripture packed with parables. These are known as the "Lost parables", not because someone found the manuscript in a decrepit cave, but because each parable in the chapter has to do with something that was lost, but was found. I personally love the resolution in the parables. In each parable the lost item is found! There is so much peace and joy in knowing that God has His grip where we feel we have lost ours. God's resolution is complete and enduring.

Let's read Luke 15 and underline the words "friends" or "neighbors" in the chapter. Dig into these Scriptures in your Bible!

"He calls together his friends and neighbors..."
"She calls together her friends and neighbors..."

Now underline in another color the words "rejoice" or "celebrate" or any form of those words in the passage.

Do you see it? Do you see the joy overflowing from each person who retrieved what was lost to them? Completely and utterly lost? Now found.

"Rejoice with me!"

"Let us eat and celebrate."

Friends are a vital aspect of our faith walk. God created the Church to be in community, not just on any given Sunday morning, but in Life Together. Laughing together, crying together, rejoicing together, eating together, and hurting together. These people in the parables are living life together.

This is a huge advantage the church has in this difficult world. Real, true, authentic community. Community surrounded and filled and connected by a God who cares greatly about the lost things of this world. A God who came into our lives, who held hands with us, who prays on our behalf, who eats with His friends. Who offers us a thousand opportunities to celebrate that joy with one another every day. God has given us a gift in one another that the world doesn't even know they are longing for – connection.

Let's call together our friends and neighbors. Let's have a lovely party. Let's celebrate. The Father has run out on the road, robes flailing around Him. He has killed the fattened calf, offered the best food and wine. We once were lost, but now we are found.

Lovely.

Exploration

Who are your favorite people to celebrate with?

How can you celebrate anew God's great love for his people, today or in the coming weeks?

commendable

week six

Commendable

Commended in Christ
Commending Ourselves
Commended by God
Commended to God
From Generation to Generation

heart verse

a verse to meditate on for the week, to post
somewhere, or to memorize:

*One generation commends your works to
another; they tell of your mighty acts.*
                    Psalm 145:4

commendable

Day 1
Commended in Christ

Commendable, or the act of commending, is not rare in Paul's Epistles. It is pretty rare to hear the word commendation or commend in our culture. You need to do something of particular honor, and it's most often military related. A commendation is a military decoration of highest honor. Saving lives, acts of heroism, an exceptional achievement.

But saving lives, acts of heroism, suffering on behalf of others, that is the language of the New Testament church. Apostles giving of their lives and themselves. People opening hearts and homes to serve. Exceptional sacrifice, struggle on behalf of another, and a ready spirit, willing to go the length, to spread the Word.

Who has gone the length for you? Who in your life has given extra for you to know Christ and His grace and mercy?

These individuals are worthy of not just honor, or thanksgiving, but this very special word – commendation.

The Greek word for commendable in Philippians 4:8 is *euphemos*. It means to be well reported of, spoken of kindly, to be reputable, and laudable. It is only found in Philippians 4:8, but the word commendable rang in my ears and I knew it was all over the New Testament letters. Why, I wondered? What was going on in history? Why is it utilized so often to describe the acts and work of those in the early church? And the overwhelming tone is similar to our use of commendation today – sacrifice.

It is an outstanding work, well reported of by others, but more than that, contextually, it is a Kingdom work of Eternal significance.

It is of no surprise to us, that which is commendable is sacrificial, because the One truly worthy of commendation is Christ, and He is above all, sacrificial.

One of my favorite Bible verses comes to mind – John 15:13:
> *Greater love has no one than this, that someone lay down his life for his friends.*

These words are spoken by Jesus, knowing exactly what he would do for us. He spoke them knowing the road He would walk, bearing sin and death and shame, but willing to do it…for you.

He is that Someone. His every step is for you.

This, friends, is so, so worthy of commendation. Worthy of telling and sharing and reporting with all zeal.

1 John 3:16 gives us a little insight into our response to His commendation in us:
> *By this we know love, that he laid down his life for us, and we ought to lay down our lives for the brothers.*

As we study what is commendable this week, let's fix our eyes on the very Commendation of God. And let Him flow out of us in the language of sacrifice.

Day 2
Commending ourselves

The title of today's study seems, at first, a complete oxymoron. How can we commend ourselves? Isn't commendation by nature wrapped up in report and reputation, which is bestowed by others?

True, and not true. Ha! In the Epistles, we see a lot of commendation happening between the brothers and sisters of the early church.
Look at Romans 16:1-2 in your Bible.

Phoebe was commended to the Romans by Paul. He asked that they welcome her, help her, provide for her.

How about 2 Corinthians 8:23-24?
(Note: the uninspired heading of this section is the Commendation of Titus.)

We are definitely invited to give commendation to one another in the church. When we know someone has a gift that can be utilized, or will be a blessing to another church or on the mission field, we can commend them and give a good report of them.

2 Corinthians 6:1-10 gives us another vantage point, one where commending ourselves is not outside the scope of God's kingdom work. I added emphasis on the commendation section for study purposes:

> *Working together with him, then, we appeal to you not to receive the grace of God in vain. For he says,*
>
> *"In a favorable time I listened to you,*
> *and in a day of salvation I have helped you."*
>
> *Behold, now is the favorable time; behold, now is the day of salvation. We put no obstacle in anyone's way, so that no fault may be found with our ministry, but as servants of God **we commend ourselves in every way**: by great endurance, in afflictions, hardships, calamities, beatings, imprisonments, riots, labors, sleepless nights, hunger; by purity, knowledge, patience, kindness, the Holy Spirit, genuine love; by truthful speech, and the power of God; with the weapons of righteousness for the right hand and for the left; through honor and dishonor, through slander and praise. We are treated as impostors, and yet are true; as unknown, and yet well known; as dying, and behold, we live; as punished, and yet not killed; as sorrowful, yet always rejoicing; as poor, yet making many rich; as having nothing, yet possessing everything.*

This verse tells us that we *report the Faith* to those around us. We give a *kind spirit to the faith* when we:

Endure
Suffer
Living pure lives
Show patience
Are kind
Are genuine
Show love
Are generous
Rejoice
Are content

Now, that's a lot of "are-s" or "be-s." Do not be afraid, sister, of not living up. That isn't the point. Our salvation is not wrapped up in our ability to live faithfully. This passage is not about what we should do, it's about what life looks like.

As Christians, we should not be surprised by affliction. Jesus tells us over and over that it's going to be our reality this side of heaven. But what this passage tells us in 2nd Corinthians, is that the afflictions, the sorrow, the struggle, all of it, does have a message, a commendation, for the world to see. He has a plan and a purpose and He WILL use it.

You are my commendation and I am yours; we live His message in and through one another. Spurring one another on. Encouraging, building up. And the message goes out. He who does this work is Faithful.

Exploration
How has or does God specifically use you uniquely, as a
commendation of His work in this world?

Thank you! Thank you for being you, and sharing Him! Fill in
your name below.

God has commended _____ for His
work.

commendable

Day 3
Commended by God

We have already talked in this study about how the world will often receive us, or the Word. Not well, for the most part. But they need it. We know that. They need us to be real and genuine. They don't need it "in their face" or harsh, or judgmental, but they do need the message of a loving God who is concerned for their welfare, and desires to lift the guilt, bear the burden, walk out of the tomb with their shame.

Honestly, sometimes, it's just hard to keep going. It's hard to be misunderstood and shut down by a world steeped in sin and reeking of hurt and distrust.

In walks 1 Corinthians 4:1-5, let's open to that text now.

> *I care very little if I am judged by you or by any human court; indeed, I do not even judge myself.* (v.3)

Perhaps this is a good memory verse. No matter what age I am, I am still struggling to outgrow both my judgment of others, and my reaction to their judgment of me. Oh, how I wish it were different! It's better than it was when I was 12. In fact, I can see a difference with every passing year and every candle added to the birthday cake. Time in the Word, and experience grants wisdom.

But we need to acknowledge the struggle. It is hard to be turned down, rejected, sent away by a world that has no use for God's justice or God's grace.

But, we are not commended by the world. We are commended by God.

What does this mean? God has written His letter of recommendation. He has signed His name and sent it to all corners of the world. He cares that it's hard, but He has fully endorsed us. We aren't sent by our own accord, or a boss, or on a family errand. We are entrusted to our task of love by a God who pours love into us. When we are tempted to be our own worst critic, the passage above reminds us that, not even our own opinion of ourselves matters in God's language. He cares what *He* thinks. And He calls us good, and worthwhile, and commendable.

Paul continues the topic in 2 Corinthians 10:12-18. Read all seven verses in your Bible. I'll highlight verse 18 below:

> *For it is not the one who commends himself who is approved, but the one whom the Lord commends.*

We can continue sharing, and inviting, and reaching, because it is the Lord who commends us. We are commendable. We are "well reported of, spoken kindly of, reputable, laudable, acceptable*" by the only One whose opinion matters.

Exploration
What experiences have you had that make it hardest for you to share your faith?

What stumbling blocks do you see around you, to the world hearing the message?

*see the interlinear Greek at biblehub.com
    (Emphasis added to ESV Bible passages by study author.)

Day 4
Commended to God

When I was a teenager my parents used to tell me over and over again, "We trust you, we just don't trust anyone else." Usually this was applied to the way people drove, or the parties I was begging to attend. My parents weren't helicopter parents. We had no strict curfew or a list of rules, but I know they were prayers and had a good deal of discernment for sniffing out a questionable situation.

The world is a dangerous place. When I became a parent myself I wrapped myself up in anxiety about who could take my child, what holes they could fall into, and what dark paths might await them. But if there is anything my parents taught me, it's that you can not control the circumstances, you can only pilot your way through it with your eyes wide open and the Word of God as your steering wheel. Eventually, the anxiety became so exhausting, that I had to give up the wrapping a little bit, and let them fly out there in the big, wide world.

Some things, we have to leave in God's hands. Actually, a great many things.

Acts 14:8-28 gives us a peek into how dark and difficult the road of life can be, but how big and bold our courage can be as we spur one another on. Pay special attention to verse 26.

So, hold the phone. Paul and Silas healed someone, then people got hacked off and tried to stone them? Yikes! They knew a thing or two about the darkness of the world around them, pressing in, threatening to devour. What is the difference between us and them? Was the church sending Paul and Silas off any less scared than we are in our world today, or with our children walking out the door tomorrow? Rather, the church around them, the people of God, who loved them dearly, remembered where they had been sent from…God, not man. They constantly commended them back to the One who is able.

God holds us close to Him. He does not let go. We may experience affliction, and hurt, and innumerable challenges, but we are held. We can encourage and commend one another to God.

I bet you have friends across the nation. I bet many of them are serving God in their little corners of the world. Take a moment and pray for one of those distant friends. They are distant in miles, but never far from your heart. Wrap them up in prayer, send them a card or a text and let them know that they are prayed for today.

Dear friend, you are commended to God. He holds you close. He hears your prayers this day.

<u>Exploration</u>
What do you think is scary in the world today?

Who did you choose to share encouragement with and commend to God? Why is that person important to you?

Day 5
From generation to generation

Psalm 145:1-9 has a special place in my heart. It's just so beautiful and declarative. And I love anything declarative, it's true. Read the passage with me.

Find the word commend and highlight that verse in your Bible if you are so willing. This commending is an amazing work of the church on earth. This is the work of every congregation and every family, and every individual - Passing down the faith from generation to generation.

We talk all the time about passing on the faith, or handing down the faith, but this passage tells us HOW. Do we commend the faith from our generation to the next? No, we commend the faith to *another* generation.

It doesn't matter the generation. We aren't married to sharing with those younger than us, or even those in the same life stage as us. We can share with those younger, and older, and all the places in between. But we do it by commending the faith. Talking highly of the faith.
Isn't it a great Faith, after all? Isn't it exactly all the things the Psalm tells us?

How has God shown Himself in your life? How have you seen, literally seen, His Greatness? What mighty acts has He done in your generation, your lifetime? What splendor do you see around you, created and sustained by Our Great God? When has He been slow to anger in your life? Where have you seen and heard and sensed His abounding Love and Mercy?

This is how we can proclaim His Name to every generation. We can declare these things and share God's work in our lives.

My friend, Sarah, just recently published a novel called *Penelope's Hope*. In it, the main character, Penelope, has a conversation with her friend, Violet. Violet exclaims to her, out of the natural disposition of her heart something like, "Isn't the Lord so good, Penelope?"

Penelope's response is not unlike that of the hurting world around us, "I can not speak for God's goodness, Violet, for I have seen but precious little of it."

Can you hear the hurt, the struggle? This is the story of so many. We are taught by the world to look for goodness in what seems good, feels good, looks good. Sometimes God works in those very things, but sometimes, often times, He works in the struggle, in the pain, in the weaving of mercy where it would not otherwise be found.

Let's declare it, friends. Let's boldly proclaim to a world in need where we can see God's goodness, God's mercy, God's abounding forgiveness and love. Let's do it gently, for the world may feel they have seen precious little of it.

Point out in conversations the Hope you are anchored in. Give a hug and remind someone of his or her value. Give a tiny piece of your story and share how God has been and worked and loved in your life, in your walk.

We have seen what is precious, not a precious little bit. Proclaim it girls. Commend away!

Exploration
Which verse stands out to you the most in the reading from Psalm 145?

What are some ideas or ways we can individually and corporately commend the faith from generation to generation?

Week Seven

Excellent

He is Excellent
Ending my battle with Proverbs 31...Excellent
Something different is Excellent
Excellent Authority
Discernment is Excellent

heart verse

a verse to meditate on for the week, to post somewhere, or to memorize:

And it is my prayer that your love may abound more and more, with knowledge and all discernment, so that you may approve what is excellent...
Philippians 1:9-10a

Day 1
He is Excellent

I know at this point that I sound like a robot. *Jesus is the answer. Jesus is Truth, Jesus is Honor, Jesus is Pure, Jesus is Loveliness, Jesus is Commendable.* But He really is the center of it all. It's so interesting to Biblically examine what all these things are in Philippians 4:8, and every single time the final answer is...

Jesus.

Every time, Jesus.

There's more to being the Alpha and Omega than being the Beginning and End. Don't forget the middle. All this space in between our birth and death, in between the discovering of who we are and where we fit. He really is in all of it. Every little detail, every piece of the untold story, every broken and mended heart.

Jesus.

And so, we should not be surprised that first and foremost, He is what is excellent. The Greek word for excellent in this passage is *arete.* It's wrapped up in virtue, moral excellence, perfection, goodness, uprightness*. It is a word, according to Thayer's Greek Lexicon, about ethics, but also thoughts, feelings, and action. In other words, it is a holistic word. Cognitive Behavioral Therapy teaches the triangle of thoughts, feelings, and behaviors, and helps people to begin reflecting on the connection between each of them. Our natural selves want things to be clean cut. "This is what I think, this over here is how I feel, and then this here is how I act," but life is not like that. Beginning to identify that what we feel affects how we act, how we think, and what we feel. We can begin to let Grace into each of those areas. Things in life are not neatly divided, and that's ok. God is working in my whole person, not just my thoughts. Not just my actions, but all of me.

Jesus did in fact give His holy excellent self, perfectly perfect, for you. His thoughts are not your thoughts; His ways are not your ways. But He is your Savior. He invades all the spaces of our lives and attributes His excellency to us, His uprightness, His virtuousness, His goodness to each of us.

We can try to change our thoughts, we can try to adjust our emotions, we can avoid certain behaviors, but His Excellent is already our Excellent.

Let's look at 2 Peter 1:3-8 for confirmation:

> *His divine power has granted to us all things that pertain to life and godliness, through the knowledge of him who called us to his own glory and excellence, by which he has granted to us his precious and very great promises, so that through them you may become partakers of the divine nature, having escaped from the corruption that is in the world because of sinful desire. For this very reason, make every effort to supplement your faith with virtue, and virtue with knowledge, and knowledge with self-control, and self-control with steadfastness, and steadfastness with godliness, and godliness with brotherly affection, and brotherly affection with love. For if these qualities are*

yours and are increasing, they keep you from being ineffective or unfruitful in the knowledge of our Lord Jesus Christ.

These qualities are yours….

He is yours. *"His divine power has granted to us all things…"* (v. 3)

Struggling with something?
Struggling with some thought? "I'm not good enough." "I'm not like her." "I need to do…"
Struggling with some feeling? Hurt, resentment, bitterness, anger, judgment.
Struggling with some action? Immobilized, guilt over sin stealing time from you, hurtful words taking over.

Precious and great promises (v.4) are yours. Forgiveness, Life, Freedom. These are all ours in Christ Jesus.

He is excellent. He lives in me.

Excellent.

Day 2
Ending my battle with Proverbs 31
...Excellent

Interestingly enough, in my Biblical search of the word excellence, Proverbs 31 kept popping up. Interesting because this is a women's Bible study, and interesting because I avoid the passage at all costs.

Proverbs 31, any proverb really, is a minefield, for the Bible study writer, in my opinion. Proverbs is wisdom literature, which means it is helpful, insightful even, but isn't meant to be always and never. I don't need to get up at 4am and sell yarn in the marketplace to be a wife of noble character (v. 13-15, interpreted by Heidi, tongue in cheek) Wisdom literature is intended to do just that - impart some broad wisdom. Think of it like talking to an older and wiser mentor woman from church. You thank God for her and discern her thoughts and ideas, but your situation may not exactly line up with her suggestions and that's ok. Complicate all of that with the inerrancy of God's Word and "ta-da!" - minefield.

However, the Proverbs 31 woman, is indeed called excellent. More than once!
Let's read together, Proverbs 31:10-31. Don't get wrapped up in it yet. Just let the words flow from the page and sit a bit.

We find excellent in verse 10 and verse 29. It's reflective of the sandwich idea again. In Hebrew, that draws attention to the reader, emphasis on one idea – She is excellent.

Most days, I feel not so excellent. I'll be honest, lately, it's been so much less than not excellent. I try to keep my family's schedule together, but I show up late everywhere. I even show up at the wrong places at the wrong times. I want to make healthy meals and forget three out of the seven ingredients at the store. It feels like my husband and children want every little piece of me and, girls, there's only so much to go around.

The Hebrew root word for excellent in this passage is *hayil*. I think it can shed some light on the subject and help us redefine Proverbs 31 and excellent for us. Praise the Lord!

Hayil is actually a masculine noun. It can mean capable, wealthy, efficient, and is reflective of strength, valour, and power. Hmmmmmm…that does not sound very feminine to me.

And maybe I'm taking this too far, maybe I'm too wrapped up in my ideas of gender roles and trying to be the mom who does it all that I'm desperate for a little scrap of Grace on the subject, but I think there is another reason this particular word is used for excellent. There are other Hebrew roots available that also reflect excellence, but God chose this one.

Maybe, just maybe, it's because we're not supposed to be Excellent.
But He is.

Christ is strong. He is capable. He is efficient. He has it all together.

I am His instrument. I go through my day. I honor Him with my lips. I let His Spirit leak out of me in the market, at my table, in bed beside my husband.

An excellent wife who can find?
A wife that reflects Christ, because He lives in me.
That's me.

That is excellent. I am excellent in Christ.

Excellent Mom. Excellent wife. Excellent me.

Exploration
What are your thoughts on other interpretations of Proverbs 31 that you have heard?

What other Bible passages can you share that you find encouraging as a wife or mom, or simply as a woman of God?

Day 3
Something different is Excellent

Sometimes there are stories, all true stories, in Scripture, that are just wild. They remind us of a powerful God and His majestic might. They signify and remind us that His thoughts are not ours, and that's ok. He is God and I am not.

Today's Bible reading is one like that. Let's open to Daniel 5. If you have your Bible out, please read all of chapter 5.

Now look at Daniel 5:30-31, 6:1-3 -
> *That very night Belshazzar the Chaldean king was killed. And Darius the Mede received the kingdom, being about sixty-two years old.*
>
> *It pleased Darius to set over the kingdom 120 satraps, to be throughout the whole kingdom; and over them three high officials, of whom Daniel was one, to whom these satraps should give account, so that the king might suffer no loss. Then this Daniel became distinguished above all the other high officials and satraps, because an excellent spirit was in him. And the king planned to set him over the whole kingdom.*

In this section of Scripture, Daniel is asked to interpret the hand and the writing on the wall. It's interesting that they always seemed to call Daniel when no one else could interpret it.

There's something different about him, they said. He knows stuff, they said. He has good insight, they said. Let's ask Daniel, they said.

All Daniel did was make himself available to be asked. He was willing to say the hard stuff, when hard stuff needed to be said. He was honest and bold, but gentle-bold, not intentionally hurtful to make a point bold.

Remember, Daniel was not given cheerful things to interpret. The writing on the wall wasn't touchy feely goodness. This is a prophecy that would bring the king's death and hand a kingdom over. But Daniel proclaimed it, truthfully. He didn't add a commentary. He made himself available when Truth was asked for. And that's one thing we can do also.

We look different. The Peace that passes understanding and Hope that anchors the soul are inside of us, leaking out. We have something different about us. We have insight into the things of the world, and the struggles of this world, that others may not have.

May we also be available.

Let's not avoid the hard conversations. Daniel's "excellent spirit" was the Spirit of the Living God inside of Him. We have that Spirit too! It may not be that we are called to interpret the writing on the wall of the king, but perhaps a friend is asking you to interpret "the writing on the wall" of their current struggle or to point out the glory of God in their current joy.

Trust Him to give you the words, at just the proper time, in the proper way. This is one reason it is so helpful to be in the Word daily. The words really do knit themselves in our heart and roll off our tongue when we need them.

Onward we go. Sharing His Light. Gentle-bold, girls! Gentle-bold.

Exploration
Share an opportunity you had to be gentle-bold with God's Word.

How can we apply gentle-boldness while using social media?

What is the most difficult topic for you to be gentle-bold about?

Day 4
Excellent authority

Honorable Ladies of the Philippians Bible Study,

How happy I am to have you join me on this journey of discussion and growth! How wonderful it is to discover the nuances of His Word, and the sweetness of His Grace through the text. Please continue on! Forge ahead in setting aside a moment each day to read, to laugh, to be challenged, and to grow up in Him, in Jesus.

May Christ's grace go before you, behind you, and in you.
Much love and affection, Heidi

Ok, so maybe we don't usually talk like that. But if I wrote you a letter today, that is what it would say. I'm so thankful to be sharing with you.

And this, friends, is how letters in the New Testament were written. People talked a little different, but not so different.

The form of the word excellent that we are going to unwrap today is associated with those in authority. It has to do with a way of addressing those of distinction by rank or order, and is often found in a letter or formal address.

The root word in Greek is *kristos* and it refers to one who is noble and/or strong, but it also is very specific as an "official epithet"

of a Roman of high rank. It's a governmental word. (Bear with me, this does have impact on our lives, I promise!)
Let's look in Acts 23:16-27, first. Please look that up in your Bible.

There is a plot against Paul by the Jews. His nephew finds out and goes to a Roman Centurion with power to impact the situation. The Centurion (Claudius) writes a letter to the governor, alerting him of the plot. Note the tone invoked in the letter by the simple use of the word *Kratisto*, or Excellency. When is it appropriate to honor someone because they hold an appropriate title? This isn't manipulation. It is recognizing and accepting authority.

So often we see Facebook posts or political comics that dishonor and poke fun at those who lead us. While, sometimes this is all in fun and our leaders are kind enough to laugh along, we need to be cautious, as Christians, to give credit where credit is due. If we want change, the Bible shows us in this passage (see also Acts 26), the appropriate way to go about it, is through speaking the Truth with respect and having care with our words.

Luke uses this form of excellent in another New Testament letter.
Read Luke 1:1-4:

> *Inasmuch as many have undertaken to compile a narrative of the things that have been accomplished among us, just as those who from the beginning were eyewitnesses and ministers of the word have delivered them to us, it seemed good to me also, having followed all things closely for some time past, to write an orderly account for you, most excellent Theophilus, that you may have certainty concerning the things you have been taught.*

This is the beginning of the Gospel of Luke, a letter to help Theophilus understand and "have certainty" about the life and work of Jesus Christ.

This gives us a new insight. We can address those that we share the Gospel with from a place of relationship and with honor and respect due to them as children of God and people He has placed in our lives. Luke knew Theophilus and knew what he had been taught. He shared further about Jesus to help him grow and learn, but he used language that lifted up. Who knows where Theophilus's theology was at, but we can guess that he didn't have it all perfect, because why else would the letter be necessary? Still, Luke calls him "most excellent." He uses the appropriate title of authority, as a way to honor the one whom he is sharing with.

We may not be writing letters or sending texts to the President or the Governor, however, we can
- Give honor to those in our society to whom honor is due…soldiers, police, political authorities, rescue personnel, teachers, pastors, etc. (Who am I missing? I know I'm missing someone! Please share in your margin!)
- Give honor to whom we share the Gospel, whether believers or unbelievers, by our language. Maybe it comes back to the gentle-bold words of Day Three. Words matter and the Holy Spirit will surely guide.

Here's a challenge: Write an actual letter! Crazy talk, right?! Dig out the notecards, find a sheet of paper, and send an encouraging note to someone today. Share Jesus, share His love, share yourself.

Dear fellow pilgrims, you are most Excellent to me.

Exploration

What groups of people or individuals do you think deserve respect because they are in a certain position? Or would you disagree that the Bible tells us anyone deserves respect, simply because of their position?

Do you have a favorite communication language? (aka do you communicate best by speaking on the phone, texting, email, writing, etc.)

Have you noticed someone else's favorite communication language?

Day 5
Discernment is Excellent

So much is excellent in our lives. We know that every good and perfect gift is from above. All the gifts we have come from the Lord. Look around you, take a moment, and praise Him by lifting up some things, some people, and some moments in life you are thankful for. Jot them down in the margin.

He is truly an Awesome God.

Today we are going to reflect on one more form of "excellent."

Philippians 1:9-11 tells us that we can approve what is excellent, we can discern that which is excellent:

> And it is my prayer that your love may abound more and more, with knowledge and all discernment, so *that you may approve what is excellent*, and so be pure and blameless for the day of Christ, filled with the fruit of righteousness that comes through Jesus Christ, to the glory and praise of God.

Again Romans 2:17-23 reflects the same phrasing:

> But if you call yourself a Jew and rely on the law and boast in God **and know his will and approve what is excellent**, because you are instructed from the law; and if you are sure that you yourself are a guide to the blind, a light to those who are in darkness, an instructor of the foolish, a

teacher of children, having in the law the embodiment of knowledge and truth— you then who teach others, do you not teach yourself? While you preach against stealing, do you steal? You who say that one must not commit adultery, do you commit adultery? You who abhor idols, do you rob temples? You who boast in the law dishonor God by breaking the law.

I added the emphasis in the ESV translations above. Can you see the similar phrases that stick?

The Greek word in these passages for excellent is *diapheronta*, which means to carry through, to show what is different, to surpass or excel. Using Scripture to interpret Scripture, we can look to the Philippians passage when we hear, "that your love may abound more and more…so that you may approve what is excellent…"

It is in love that we are able to see what is excellent.

When we look at everything around us, we look with the rose colored glasses of God's love for His people. Occasionally, our zeal for the law, our legalism for things that are excellent, and righteous even, blind us to being able to see what is Christ. Certainly the Gospel cannot be understood apart from the Law, but we can be so wrapped up in how we *think* the law or the gospel should look, that we miss it standing in front of us. Let's let our discernment be Christ's discernment in us, not our ideas about what is right and wrong, but firmly planted in God's Justice and God's Grace, revealed in His Word.

Romans 2:21 above, asks, *"you then who teach others, do you not teach yourself?"*

*It is only in being the constant learner that we can
discern what is excellent.*

We approve what is excellent by sitting as Mary sat at Jesus's
feet, by letting Grace sweep over us; letting dishes stay
unwashed and work left undone. We daily are invited to pick up
the Word, and use a moment to bask in His purity, His goodness,
and His Words of Excellence.

Excellence in the passages today is discerned in the daily life
with Christ. It's not found in the Sunday morning box we check,
but in the authenticity of the journey, because we firmly believe
in an authentic God, and He gives us His authentic Word to learn
and grow and love.

What, therefore, is excellent to you? What do you see around you
that surpasses because it is of Him?

That may be your church (It is excellent! He created it!); It may
also be your garden; it may be the laughter in your home; or the
tears of a friend shed over a shared life. It changes our idea of
what is excellent, because to be excellent, it simply needs to be
touched by Him, redeemed by His Grace.

Go and discern, ladies. We have something a little different to
share. Something that will carry us through. This life, this
walk...excellent.

<u>Exploration</u>
What in your life currently needs discernment?

How do you think you learn best? (listening, discussing, seeing pictures or print, writing, etc.)

*occasional emphasis added to Scripture texts by author through bold or italic markings

week eight

Worthy of Praise

If the shoe fits…Praise it!
He saves again and again – Praiseworthy!
The struggle – worthy of Praise…
Don't Praise a book by its cover
Praises for endings, along with new beginnings

heart verse

a verse to meditate on for the week, to post
somewhere, or to memorize:

Let the peoples praise you, O God;
let all the peoples praise you!
Psalm 67:5

Day 1
If the shoe fits...

Can you believe it? This is our last week of study, girls! We did it! At the end of a Bible study I always feel a surreal sense of completion. Like the Spirit is cheering us along at the end of the race. "On to the finish line!" He shouts! It's just a good reminder of the not-yet-finished race we run in life, but also a reminder that it is in fact finished. Jesus completed that good work, but we get to be a part of the richness of it together, by running the race and sharing the Word together, in our time in history.

Worthy of praise is a GREAT wrap up of all things true, honorable, just, pure, lovely, commendable, and excellent. It's convenient, because I feel like in the last seven weeks, we have in fact studied all things worthy of praise.

- Speaking and hearing Truth – worthy of praise.
- Giving and receiving Honor – worthy of praise.
- Justice poured out by a Gracious God – worthy of praise.
- Purity in Life, lived in Christ – worthy of praise.
- Lovely creation, lovely sacrifice – worthy of praise.
- Commendable people, commendable promises – worthy of praise.
- Excellent Savior, excellent discernment – worthy of praise.

The Greek for worthy of praise in Philippians 4:8 is *epainos*. This means that it is "fitting for praise", it's accurate praise, enthusiastic praise, appropriate praise and appropriate fame*. There is a fair amount of emphasis on the idea of praise that fits, or is appropriate.

I think this gives us a good window into praise in our current cultural context. We can throw around accolades and honor all kinds of things as "worthy of praise" but do we mean it? Is it really worthy?

I'm a superlative kind of person. I like things big, with multiple exclamation points, and a few emoticons. My husband always brings me down to Earth. Early in our marriage, he was disturbed by my use of the phrase, "Awesome!"
I used it for everything.

"Isn't this food awesome!"
"Love that movie. It's awesome!"
"You are awesome!"
"Time for bed…awesome!"

You may laugh, but maybe only because you're a little guilty too. ;) In our culture words like epic and massive are used for everything in youth culture and then quickly catch on in the adult world. The online Urban Dictionary's definition for epic is actually "the most overused word ever." (Don't look it up because there's a fair amount of cursing in the post. Be forewarned.)

One way we can shine a little light seems obvious to me, but a little easier said than done. Let's save the superlatives for things worthy of superlatives. And the praise, for things actually worthy of praise.

And wouldn't you know, when you get down to it, things worthy of praise are always things associated with God.

First, the section of Scripture that uses the word Praise over and over and over again, Psalm 67:

> *May God be gracious to us and bless us*
> *and make his face to shine upon us, Selah*
> *that your way may be known on earth,*
> *your saving power among all nations.*
> *Let the peoples praise you, O God;*
> *let all the peoples praise you!*
> *Let the nations be glad and sing for joy,*
> *for you judge the peoples with equity*
> *and guide the nations upon earth. Selah*
> *Let the peoples praise you, O God;*
> *let all the peoples praise you!*
> *The earth has yielded its increase;*
> *God, our God, shall bless us.*
> *God shall bless us;*
> *let all the ends of the earth fear him!*

"That your way may be known on the earth…" This is the point of praise. When we praise our children, let us lift it up to the God who works in them. When we praise a food, let it be because He made the seed grow (v. 6). When we praise a form of entertainment, let it be because He has given us laughter and joy and rest. But let it be worthy.

Seem like a bit much?

1 Peter 2:15-17, gives us a little insight into what is worthy of praise. Let's look that one up in our Bibles.

When we call attention to what is actually fitting for praise, we can silence that which is not. And, instead of fighting evil with words of anger and frustration, we can offer up a praise for what is worthy of praise. We can spend our whole lives filling our Facebook posts fighting things that make us angry, or talking to people about Hollywood sensations and the latest gossip. Or we can fill a feed and a conversation with something worthy.

The shoe fits, for sure. I'm a sinner. My words and my time get eaten up and used in all kinds of ways that are not worthy of praise. But He is completely and utterly worthy. He gives us shoes of forgiveness and mercy that fit just right. He also gives us the Spirit-filled shoes in our baptism that give us a new mouthpiece when we are sorely in need of one.

The shoe fits, for sure. He is worthy. Always has been. Always will be.
Let the peoples praise you, O God. Let all the peoples praise you! Let me be one of them.

Exploration
What are some of the things you would praise God for, right now? List at least 5.

What are some of the hardest conversations for you, and the hardest conversations to avoid?

Day 2
He saves me, and saves me, and saves me some more...

Jesus is a once-and-for-all kind of God. He tells us in His Word that the battle is over, the fight has been won. The cross paid the full price for our sin. The Resurrection gave us eternal life. It is finished, it is done. (See Romans 8:37-39, John 16:33)

But he's also an everyday kind of God, a not-quite-done-with-me God. (See Philippians 1:4-6, 2 Timothy 4:6-8) We are still in this race, still slapping our armor on each day. He is still working out His plan in our lives, every day.

2 Samuel 22 is filled with David's words of exultation and thanksgiving for God's salvation. This beautiful testimony to God's saving action in our lives is repeated again in Psalm 18. And it is indeed worthy of repeat. Let's read at least 2 Samuel 22:1-7. Feel free to look up the whole chapter. It's beautiful!

David was miraculously saved from Saul's torment of him, through an enemy. God's ways of rescue and salvation are ceaselessly amazing. He used a manger and a cross to save us. Who would have seen that coming?

But David's days of battle were far from over with Saul's death. 2 Samuel is packed with battles and there is a reason that the passage above goes on for 51 more verses! God continued to save David, to shelter and protect him, as well as to discipline and forgive him, for His whole life, day in and day out.

That is the message of 2 Samuel 22 and Psalm 18 – an almost endless praise for the saving works of God, both those done and those he continues to do.

What has God saved you from?

Maybe you were premature at birth, maybe you were in a terrible auto accident, maybe adolescence almost got the best of you. Maybe hopelessness seeped in at one point in your life, maybe you are struggling with the loss of a child. Perhaps mental illness, anxiety, or depression has walked in your front door. Wherever you have been and whatever battles lie ahead, He is the same Savior.

He saves us yesterday, today, and tomorrow. He died once for all, but we are daily made new.

Lord God, I don't know what battle each person faces, but I pray for each and every battle. Jesus, you are our salvation. You rescue, you heal, you set us on a solid rock. We praise you today. Thank you for your goodness, your love, and your mercy. In Jesus name, Amen.

He's not done with you yet, sister!

<u>Exploration</u>
What battles or situations do you remember about David's life?

How do they testify individually to the saving grace of God?

What has God saved you from and what do you need refuge from currently?

Day 3
The struggle is worthy of Praise

Most days I see so much beauty in the world. Fall colors, corn grown ripe for the harvest out my back window, faces of people I love.

Most days I also see ugly. Hard stuff. Hurtful stuff. Disease. Tumult. The gunk of life.

1 Peter 1:6-9 tells us about the gunk of life:
> *In this you rejoice, though now for a little while, if necessary, you have been grieved by various trials, so that the tested genuineness of your faith—more precious than gold that perishes though it is tested by fire—may be found to result in praise and glory and honor at the revelation of Jesus Christ. Though you have not seen him, you love him. Though you do not now see him, you believe in him and rejoice with joy that is inexpressible and filled with glory, obtaining the outcome of your faith, the salvation of your souls.*

So much of life is spent trying to avoid the struggle. I am a guilty party. Christian artist, Mat Kearney, has a song, "Air I Breathe." I could not figure out for the life of me, what it was in the song that I was drawn to, what the lyrics meant. Then, I sat down to write this Bible study and the lyrics tumbled around my head, uninvited. There are lyrics that stick out to me about fights we are unable to win and white flags that need to be thrown down. Initially, I thought this song was about my youth, about running from God and Him finding me in every little crevice I hid, but then I realized that I have the same fight in me daily. My sinner saint self is wrestling, fighting, struggling, everyday.

In addition to that though, I completely relate to the idea that so often we are fighting against the good things God wants to do in our lives, simply because it may not look "good" to us. In fact, it may look horrible to us. It may look like cancer, or Bipolar, or ugly friendships. I am constantly fighting back, angry at things that cause discomfort, sorrow, and struggle. God hates disease and sickness and all those things that come from sin in the world, as much as we do, probably more. But His thoughts are also not our thoughts, His ways, not our ways.

He will use them. He will use them in a way that we never could imagine.

1st Peter tells us that He will use them for His praise. Struggles, worthy of praise?! Say it isn't so!

I'm not sure I could have heard this message in the struggle. But this is a truth we can take in and store up in our heart, so that when the struggle comes, we can sit in it, wrestle with it, even call it good, when it feels like So. Much. Struggle.

There's another guy who knew about the struggle.
Let's read Genesis 32:22-31.

When the struggle comes, everything we have is stripped bare. We are left standing alone on the bank. God gives us an open invitation to wrestle with him, to work it out in prayer and frustration and anger and sorrow. What is your hip joint? What is the struggle in your life that has left you limping, or that you fear is coming and you're terrified of?

Here's a challenge. Praise Him, not in spite of the struggle, but because of it. Praise him for the limp. My limp is living with mental illness in my house. Wrestling with anxiety. Shattered missionary dreams.

How can I begin to find these things praiseworthy?

I can, because He is in every little piece of them.

In fact, what I have learned is that in my weakness, in my wrestling, He is more clear than ever. His Grace and Salvation and Glory wash over me, when at other times they would go ignored. I am reminded that God baptized me in that river that I stand beside. He will not leave His work incomplete. I hold tight to His promise in those waters. And so I can wrestle and be refined, and praise His name in the gunk and muck and thick of it.

Struggle. The truth is, it's worthy of praise.

Exploration

What's the hardest part of struggle- in general, or for you personally?

What struggles can you identify as praiseworthy, whether your own or in the world around you?

What have you learned in times of weakness?

Day 4
Don't Praise a book by its cover...

My mama taught me early on that you can't judge a book by it's cover. This rule goes for actual books, as well as people, and stuff you need to buy, and life situations, and all kinds of things.

I like to read. A lot. I love the new book shelf at the library. Glossy and perfect hardcover marvelousness, but half the time I open the book and it's slightly or mostly trashy, has all kinds of sexual verbiage, some not-so-minor cursing, concealing a terribly underdeveloped plot and weak characters. I sound really judgmental, authors, I apologize ahead of time.

The reality is, a glossy, shiny, clever book cover can not make a book worthwhile to read. Some books, I have even stopped reading before chapter one was finished.

We are like this too. We can be glossy in appearance. Maybe this looks like we put on our makeup and did our hair, or maybe we are the woman who "has it all together" or speaks kind and tender things to the neighbor and checks on church members. We can recite the catechism. We want to sound good, look good. We like to feel like we know what we are talking about and look like we know what we are doing.

None of these things are bad, in and of themselves. In fact, most of what I listed above are really good and can be very genuine fruits of a life lived in mercy and grace.

Romans 2:25-29 warns us, though, that none of what it "looks like" matters. See what it has to say in your Bible.

I have the problem that I *can* set aside what I'm "supposed" to look like each day and be the real me, but I often backtrack and lay in bed at night wondering what people thought of me. Satan uses even my desire to share genuine faith as a torment for me to believe that this is what matters...whether people think I'm genuine!

It's sounds a mite ridiculous, I know. So I rest in Truth.

"His praise is not from man but from God."

God will do His work. His Spirit shines out whether my cover is dusty and struggling, "appears genuine", or I'm having an all out good day. God's praise is praiseworthy. Men's praise, man's ideas of what I am or do or confess, not praiseworthy. In the words of Taylor Swift, "Shake it off." Shake off what is outward, what people think and perceive of you. Focus on the heart, the One residing there. He is praiseworthy.

One day we will hear His praise of a life well lived in Him – "Well done good and faithful servant." (Matthew 23:25) Be His Living Book now. His is the praise that matters.

Exploration

What kind of praise and acclamation do you struggle with seeking?

What praise or acclamation can you share about God's work
a) as our Savior on the cross and

b) lived out in your life in the last week?

Day 5
Praises for endings,
as well as new beginnings

We've come to the last day. This is it. I can hardly believe it. Philippians 4:8, 8 weeks of study, wrapped up and tucked in our hearts. That is a beautiful thing.

There is so much to praise Him for, and whether you are in a joyous season or in a dark valley, there is room to praise Him. It may not look and feel like the same praise. In fact, it may not "feel" like anything at all. It may be forced and rote; It may be exuberant and uninhibited, but that's the beauty of God's promises…He doesn't slap legalistic expectations on us. He leaves it open to relationship and growth and *He sees just as much worth in the praise that falls as tears from our eyes, as He does the song of praise on our lips.*

Maybe you are in the joy place. I had no problem finding Bible verses about praising the Lord. He is so worthy! The Word is filled with trumpets, and dancing, and the rocks crying out. Psalm 98 speaks perfect Truth. It's worth the read. Write your favorite verse from it in the margin.

In other Scriptures, Ephesians 1:3-14 repeats the phrase "to the praise of His glory" three times while reminding the reader of His marvelous salvation. Revelation 5 palpitates with the praises of the Saints and the Universe. David dances before God who brought victory and His presence back to His people.

It is not hard to find a Bible verse about praising the Lord.

But maybe that's not your place. Maybe the road is Psalm 23 dark in the valley of the shadow. You know Truth. You stand on Truth. This is not a problem. But your praise has left you. The Christian radio station can talk a good talk about praising Him in the storm with hands lifted high, but sometimes we need an Aaron to raise them, because they feel like rocks today.

I found stored away in the Psalms a precious verse that reminds us that praise may look a lot different than we ever imagined.

This was a hard lesson for me, only learned on a dark and painful road. Dreams blown up in smoke, illness tearing at my children, and everything I thought was solid in my life melting away.

I wept in church. I wept quiet tears in my bed at night. I wept til the well ran dry and then I wept some more. In Adult Bible Study one Sunday morning this verse came up. Let's back up a few pages to Psalm 56: 1-8 –

> *Be gracious to me, O God, for man tramples on me;*
> *all day long an attacker oppresses me;*
> *my enemies trample on me all day long,*
> *for many attack me proudly.*
> *When I am afraid,*
> *I put my trust in you.*
> *In God, whose word I praise,*
> *in God I trust; I shall not be afraid.*
> *What can flesh do to me?*
> *All day long they injure my cause;*[a]
> *all their thoughts are against me for evil.*

They stir up strife, they lurk;
* they watch my steps,*
* as they have waited for my life.*
For their crime will they escape?
* In wrath cast down the peoples, O God!*
You have kept count of my tossings;
** put my tears in your bottle.**
Are they not in your book?

My tears, He collects each and every one in His bottle. At first, when I heard this verse, I was angry. Why does God want my tears? Why? What kind of morbid God collects my tears and hoards them. Why doesn't He step in instead? Do something useful?!

Obviously, God's plans are much greater than man can even behold. At that moment, I didn't care. What God slowly revealed to my heart tenderly, in His Word, was that He collects my tears and holds them sacred, because they are just as much praise to Him as my joy and laughter. They honor Him because they seek Him. Tears are so often private or at the very least, very, very personal. They are a thing between you and God in those dark moments. They bind us to people who are willing to cry with us, but when the pain cuts deep, our tears bring us before a Creator who is present, who collects them and stores them in His Book of Life, because they are beautiful and worth keeping.

So, whatever your praise place today -- Cry out to Him! Praise Him with your voice, praise Him with pen on paper, praise Him in your conversation, and praise Him with those tears.

He alone is purely and truly and excellently and justly and commendably... Worthy of Praise!

<u>Exploration</u>
What is your favorite way to praise the Lord?

In what times have you found yourself praising in a way you never imagined?

What are some encouragements we can share with those who are worn out, sad, or discouraged?

Thank you for studying the Word with me! If you have any thoughts, questions, or would like permission to copy this booklet, please contact the author, Deaconess Heidi Goehmann, MSW, LSW at hlgoehmann@gmail.com or ilovemyshepherd.com. I would love to hear from you!

A heart full of gratitude goes out to my editing friends, particularly Sarah Baughman, my number one encourager and sister of my heart; to Dave for always listening to hours of ideas so patiently; and Melissa Sue Photo in Ohio for the cover design and selflessly utilizing her gifts so often, for the glory of God.

Made in the USA
Coppell, TX
08 April 2021